I'll Gather My Geese

I'll Gather My Geese

Hallie Crawford Stillwell

Texas A&M University Press
College Station

The paper used in this book meets the minimum requirements
of the American National Standard for Permanence
of Paper for Printed Library Materials, Z39.48-1984.
Binding materials have been chosen for durability.

LIBRARY OF CONGRESS CATALOGING-IN-PUBLICATION DATA

Stillwell, Hallie Crawford, 1897–
    I'll gather my geese / Hallie Crawford Stillwell. —
1st ed.
        p.   cm.
    ISBN 0-89096-478-5
    1. Ranch life—Texas—Marathon Region—
History—20th century. 2. Marathon Region (Tex.)—
Social life and customs. 3. Stillwell, Hallie Crawford,
1987– . 4. Marathon Region (Tex.)—Biography.
5. Ranchers' wives—Texas—Marathon Region—
Biography. I. Title.
F394.M295S75   1991
976.4′932—dc20   90-47692
                                           CIP

I dedicate this book
to the loving memory of my husband,
Roy Stillwell,
and to my children,
Son, Dadie, and Guy.

Contents

Illustrations

Preface

WHEN writing this book I did not aspire to write a masterpiece. I wanted only to leave with my children and grandchildren something about my life on the raw frontier of Texas. My small role in "taming the West" was different from that of other women who lived there because of the many years I spent in the saddle playing an active part in the cattle business.

I have written about things that I experienced personally: the Pancho Villa revolution and raids along the Rio Grande, traveling on a boarded highway, crossing raging water at flood stage on a barge, living through the Spanish influenza, surviving the 1929 financial crash, living through the drought of the thirties, tending my family in sickness and through accidents, keeping the home fires burning in spite of adverse conditions, and holding onto land that I cherished. These are experiences I know about or was told about by my husband, Roy. My research is limited due to a lack of documentation in the far West Texas area during much of my life on this frontier. I had no reason to doubt Roy, and therefore I offer to you, the reader, what I believe to be true or what I know to be true based on what I was told or experienced.

I want to thank all those who inspired me to write this book. My children and grandchildren were always supportive of me, urging me to get on with it. Also, I want to thank my many friends who said, "Hallie, you should write a book." Thanks also to my granddaughter Brenda Trudeau who worked many hours typing and putting this manuscript on the computer; to Dr. Elton Miles, a retired English professor of Sul Ross State University in Alpine, for reading the manuscript and making valuable suggestions; to Inda Benson and Lisa Beaumont for reading it and giving me courage when I needed it; and the group of friends who are members of the Alpine Book Club for their encouragement. And a special thank you goes to my cousin Betty Heath for personally taking this manuscript to the Texas A&M University Press.

I'll Gather My Geese

The Bride

IT was July 29, 1918. I was a nervous bride-to-be and twenty years old. I should have been excited and elated that the handsomest and most eligible bachelor around had proposed marriage, but instead I could only think of Papa's words: "He's too old for you and he hasn't led a proper life. That man drinks and gambles too much. He's just not suitable for you, daughter!"

Still, I was a determined woman even at that young age. I chose to marry Roy Stillwell against Mama's and Papa's words of advice. I had too much respect for my parents to blatantly defy them, so Roy and I just climbed into his Hudson Super-6, drove to the Brewster County Court House, got our marriage license, and imposed on my cousin, Sadie Crawford Harrington. After a quick ceremony at her house, we drove to Marathon and boarded the train for San Antonio, where we would spend our honeymoon at the Gunter Hotel.

Four days later we left San Antonio and headed home, where I was to present my new husband to Mama and Papa. I was anxious and apprehensive when we left the train station in Marathon. The drive from Marathon to Alpine was quiet as both of us anticipated the worst reaction from my parents.

We drove up to my home and walked inside. The family was sitting at the dinner table. I stumbled over my words very quickly. "Mama and Papa, Roy and I are married!" Roy and I stood side by side and waited.

After a few moments of tense silence, Papa rose and spoke, "Well, the die is cast! Y'all better sit down and have some supper."

From that day forward, Roy was a member of my family. Mama and Papa never looked back and never treated Roy any worse than any other member of my family. I had anticipated the worst and had gotten what I had really hoped for, acceptance of Roy by my mother and father.

My father did question Roy extensively about our lives together. He asked Roy, "Are you going to be living in your house in Marathon?"

Roy was prompt in his reply. "I own that house in Marathon, but the ranch is my home and Hallie will be living on the ranch with me. We will keep the house in town as a place to come when we need to be in town, which should not be very often."

I knew Papa was not any too happy about my living that far from town, especially in a place so close to the Mexican border. Not only was Pancho Villa a renowned raider but many Mexicans used his name as their scapegoat when they raided isolated ranches along the Rio Grande. Papa frowned, but only warned: "Just take good care of her."

Once we had visited with family and friends for a few days, Roy decided that we had better head for his ranch, a ride some seventy-five miles from Alpine and an all-day drive. As we rode along I could tell that Roy was somewhat apprehensive. He was polite and pointed out many interesting names and places along the way. I absorbed the beautiful surroundings and knew that I would be happy around the mountains and cacti that protected the rough terrain. Once we were within ten miles of the ranch, Roy began to get quiet and looked quite concerned. I finally asked. "Roy is something bothering you?"

"Well, Hallie, there has never been a woman living on my ranch. The cowhands and I have always taken care of everything and never felt we needed a woman. Now, these men are good men but they may need a while to get used to you."

As we drove up to the ranch house, I saw three rough-looking cowboys leaning up against a brush arbor that was attached to a tiny shack that was the ranch headquarters. I really hadn't expected much but I was somewhat surprised at its size, one room about twelve feet by sixteen feet. Still I kept my chin up.

Roy, being quite a gentleman, slid out of the car and came around to open my door. He allowed me to get out and then pointed toward the tiny house. "This is it!"

I started toward the house with Roy right behind me.

"Hell, that woman schoolteacher won't last six months down here in this Godforsaken country" was the remark that I heard from one of the ranch hands as Roy and I made our way toward the arbor. I really did not pay too much attention to this remark because I knew that it was one I was not supposed to hear. Roy either did not hear it or pretended not to hear it, and we walked up to the trio awaiting us.

The men showed respect by removing their hats and extending their hands, but I felt their discontent. They stood quietly under the arbor while Roy ushered me inside. It did not take me long to survey the domain. The room contained a small wood cookstove with a smoke-blackened coffee pot, a huge black iron teakettle, and a few pots and pans. There was a small cabinet (usually referred to as a safe) and on it was a shelf where a water bucket and gourd dipper stood. Also in the room were one table, one chair, two wooden benches, and only one bedroll, a mass of rolled-up quilts wrapped in a tarp in a corner. I then realized that I would have to share that cowboy bedroll with Roy, and that it would be our bed.

"Come on in, boys, let's fix a bite of supper," called Roy to the men waiting impatiently outside, as he immediately began to scrape ashes out of the stove.

I sat in a chair as those clumsy cowboys stomped into the house and began to cook our supper. Little did I know how efficient at camp cooking they were. The more they worked, the more in the way I felt. As those earlier words from the cowboys echoed through my mind, I became more determined to stay. I wanted desperately to make a go of my marriage regardless of the stinging remarks these men had made.

As I sat at the table to have my first meal in my new home, I again felt the coldness of the ranch hands' reception. They were ignoring me, and Roy was bending over backwards to melt the icy atmosphere. I smiled at the hands' crude remarks and complimented the cooks. Not one of the three icebergs thawed that evening.

The only conversation consisted of shallow cutting remarks. "I reckon you'll be a goin' back to town most of the time," Lee said as he gathered the tin plates, three-pronged forks, and case knives to wash.

"No, I expect to live here with Roy, or I wouldn't have married him," I replied.

"It's no fittin' place fer a woman," mumbled Jona as he headed for the door.

"We have work ahead of us tomorrow, boys. See you in the morning," Roy said as he untied the bedroll, spread it on the floor, and prepared our bed for the night.

I watched as the three taciturn men picked up their bedrolls stacked under the arbor and retired to the barn. I was glad to have them out of my sight. They had been acting as if they owned Roy, I thought. I turned to say something to Roy and found him already in the bedroll. I fumbled around for awhile, got myself ready for bed, and rolled in next to him.

"They will never own me," I muttered without thinking.

Roy, already half asleep, asked what I had said.

"Nothing, absolutely nothing," I whispered.

5

JACKSON,   WACO.

1. Hallie Crawford, one year old

I curled up in the bedroll and thought about the peaceful night, warm with a light stir of a cool breeze. I heard the squeak of the wooden wheel on the windmill as it turned. Once in a while, I heard a coyote yip in the distance or a mother cow bawling for her calf. The hypnotic rhythm of the windmill should have put me to sleep, but it didn't. The remarks I had overheard that evening were still too fresh on my mind. My hipbones ached as I turned from side to side attempting to get comfortable. My mind remained active. I wondered what my role as a pioneer ranch wife would be like. This man lying next to me had had such a different life from mine.

As I mused on the blending of my life and his, my thoughts traveled backwards. I had been born in Waco, Texas, on October 20, 1897, and at the age of one year, my parents, Guy and Nancy Crawford, moved me, my brother Frank, and my sister Mabel to the San Angelo

6

2. Wedding picture, Nancy Montgomery and Alvin Guy Crawford (Hallie's parents)

area. As we children grew, my parents became concerned about our
education and better opportunities for our family. With these two aims
in mind, we made five moves in twelve years, during which time our
family had grown to include another brother, Alvin, and another sister, Lovenia. All of our moves were in West Texas except for a three-
year period of homesteading in the territory of New Mexico. Alvin had
been born in 1900 in Ozona, where we had lived for two years, and
Lovenia was born in 1905 in San Angelo, where we had also resided.
Included in this family was my father's sister, Lambe, who had made
her home with us always. Even though our family was large, my father never hesitated to make a move if he felt that it would be for the
betterment of our family.

3. Ruby Burcham (friend), Hallie, and Sadie (cousin) after a horseback ride, 1913

Moves during this era were hard and we had to move in covered wagons. In preparation for a journey, wagon wheels had to be soaked in hot linseed oil, hubs greased, and wagon beds repaired. We spent several days on the road as we traveled to each new place. And with each new home, we faced a new set of hardships, something Aunt Lambe was always good at predicting. She seemed to have a nose for catastrophe.

The last move I made with my family was in 1910 to Alpine, Brewster County, Texas. It didn't take long for my parents to realize that Alpine met their needs. It offered opportunities to make a good living, the school system was good, and Uncle Jim Crawford (my father's brother) and his family also lived there. Because of the advantages offered in Alpine, particularly in education, my father settled us there

8

4. Hallie Crawford, high school graduation picture, 1916

and sent all of us children to school except for Frank, who was needed to help with my father's business, a local grocery store.

I started school in Alpine as a sixth grader, and by the time I graduated from Alpine High School in 1916, I not only had my high school diploma but also my teaching certificate. I had completed six weeks of training at the Normal School for Teachers and had taken and passed the state examinations, allowing me certification to teach in the state of Texas.

There were few jobs for women during these years, and teaching was certainly the most respectable job for a woman in the West Texas area. I had heard that there was a vacancy in Presidio, and I quickly wrote a letter to the president of the Board of Trustees of the Presidio Common School. In a short time, I was informed that I had a teaching job.

Presidio was largely populated by Texans of Mexican descent. Most of these people had fled Mexico seeking protection from Pancho Villa and his raiders. Pancho Villa and his army had recently captured Ojinaga, Mexico, just across the Rio Grande from Presidio, and all of Mexico was in a rebellion, causing many hardships within the country and a torn-up government.

My father thought this place was too dangerous for a young lady. He didn't want me to go, and stressed this point often.

"Daughter, I think you're going on a wild goose chase," he said.

I finally replied somewhat flippantly, "Then I'll gather my geese." Even though my father disapproved of my going to Presidio, I armed myself with a six-shooter, my father's favorite and most dependable weapon and one he was very glad to lend me, took my teaching certificate, and headed for Presidio.

When I arrived in Presidio, I found the days hot, the sand deep, the Mexicans strange, and the U.S. soldiers curious about an Anglo girl moving there. There was only one other white girl there, Alice Gourley, who was also a teacher. These soldiers were stationed there to protect the U.S. border and often wondered at our wanting to teach in such a dangerous setting. The lodgings provided for Alice and me were makeshift and not very comfortable. After a short time there, I sent for my sister Mabel to take a teaching position in the school. She, Alice, and I set up housekeeping together, and this made our living there more satisfactory and my stay more pleasant. Although the environment was harsh I was not a quitter, and the dangerous happenings there could not keep me from my school and my sweet little children.

Most of my days in this village were spent working with the children, preparing lessons, or cleaning the schoolhouse. In the evenings, the three of us would often visit with the Texas Rangers and customs agents stationed there. We attended church on Sundays and once a week we were able to watch a silent movie. I never remember being bored or discontented.

Mabel had to walk three miles to her school and I really felt sorry for her. I decided to help her out. I put out word that I wanted to buy

5. Couple Hallie rented from in Presidio, 1916

a horse, and before long a Mexican approached me. He told me that he had a horse to sell and wanted twenty-two dollars for it. I paid for the horse and led him to our cabin, where I presented him to Mabel. She was excited that she would not have to walk so far any longer.

Mabel got up every morning and rode that horse to and from school for about a month. Then, one day, two customs agents appeared at our door asking about the horse outside and wanting to know who owned it.

Of course, I proudly claimed ownership.

"Lady, you bought a 'wet horse'!" stated the agents, meaning that I had bought a horse that had been brought illegally from Mexico.

I did not understand what he was talking about at first. I was surprised to find out that the horse had been brought from Mexico without proper documents. The agents told me that they would have to seize my animal. We were all depressed about the loss of the horse and Mabel's means of transportation to her school.

I think those agents felt sorry for me and they gave me twenty-five dollars for the horse. They explained that the government was paying for the horse and would return it to Mexico. I knew in my heart that those men created that purse for me, and I will never forget them.

The Mexican people of Presidio were very respectful, as were most of the soldiers. Of course, there can always be one "bad apple in the barrel" and I had to come across that one soldier. One night, around midnight, I was sound asleep. Alice awakened me abruptly, whispering that someone was trying to break into our cabin. I rushed to the front door and called to some passing soldiers who were on patrol. They heard our story, began a search, and found a young soldier boy hiding in a haystack behind our place. That soldier was promptly placed in the guardhouse, and the next day was tried and sentenced to six months in confinement. That soldier's commanding officer came by the next day and apologized for the soldier's bad behavior. He assured us that the soldiers were there to protect us and gave us a strong sense of security. After that we felt much more comfortable.

There was seldom any routine in Presidio, and we were forced to adjust quickly to changes. Many times during that year in Presidio, the Mexicans from Ojinaga heard rumors of Pancho Villa planning a raid on the village. People packed up their families, friends, and belongings and came to Presidio, where they sought refuge. There were nights when we were awakened to the sounds of babies crying, women fussing, and feet rustling along the streets. We knew then that the rumors were flying. Each time the Mexicans moved to Presidio, the three of us had to move to the custom agent's house that was positioned in the center of the fort. We hated to have to move so quickly from our own cabin, but the commanding officer assured us that it was for our own protection.

The times were rough. To get to my school, I had to walk half a mile in deep sand in heat that often soared above a hundred degrees Fahrenheit. I also had to wear my father's gun to school every day. On my way home from school one day, two drunk soldiers began to follow me. I knew that they were not just taking a walk. I quickened my pace and they did too. I took off running and they quickly came after me. I never thought of using my gun; I only thought of getting away. I probably ran faster that day than I ever ran in my whole life, and I did outrun them. When I finally got to our cabin I stormed inside and bolted our door. I knew that the only reason that I got away from them was because they were so drunk. I learned much during that one year, and the experiences prepared me for many hardships I later faced in life.

The following year, 1917, I moved to Marathon, Texas, to teach where the dangers were fewer. This move made my father very happy, but I was not overly excited until I met a tall, handsome cowboy who drove a Hudson Super-6. At this time, I was boarding with the Louie Ritchey family. The Ritcheys were Roy's friends, and they invited him to attend a dance with us at "Punkin Center" (a lone little school-house) just north of town. I danced with Roy until the sun was peeking over the mountains early the next morning. I had the most wonderful time of my life, and Marathon became a much brighter place in which to teach and live.

After that one evening of dancing and fun, Roy invited me for automobile rides (a luxury of that time), picnics, and all social functions held in Marathon. Roy, being old-fashioned, believed that the way to a woman's heart was through a serenade and candy. Roy could not sing or play the guitar, but he found Ira Shely, a fiddler, and a blind Mexican who accompanied Ira with a guitar, to sing to me outside my window. I began to find myself awakening in the middle of the night to melodious love songs. I would be arisen from a deep sleep by the music of my favorite songs, "Listen to the Mockingbird" and "The Reagan Waltz." At that point, I knew that Roy Stillwell was the most dashing, handsome, and romantic man in the country, or at least knew what made my heart do "flip-flops." He was twenty years my senior, but this made no difference and I found myself completely in love. After such fine courting, Roy and I became engaged for a short time: four months.

As I reminisced over these wonderful memories, the hard floor softened and Roy's peaceful breathing began to relax me. As I lay in my new home and listened to the harmonious sounds around the ranch, I knew that I had begun to "gather my geese."

Stillwell Ranch was and is located twenty-two miles north of the Rio Grande as it flows between Texas and Mexico. It is forty-six miles from Marathon, the nearest town. When Roy first brought me to this ranch, it consisted of three hundred sections of open range and small traps (pastures for holding livestock) here and there. This was the last frontier of Texas; it became known as the Big Bend country. I knew that I would come to love the land although it was hot, sandy, and even lonely at times.

As I settled more comfortably in our bedroll I thought of my arrival at the ranch and how I had looked forward to a new life. I thought of the Maravillas Creek and how Roy told me that the creek had water in it only when it rained, which wasn't often. There were rocky mountains, low cactus-covered hills, and dagger flats. This was a land of stark beauty. I knew it was also a land of danger. I began to think about this environment that I knew I loved already. I knew that Roy would protect me from the dangers and teach me how to protect myself. I was ready to accept my responsibilities as his wife and for the ranch. We could and would make Stillwell Ranch what we wanted it to be if we worked together.

I did dwell on the fact that Pancho Villa and his raiders were rampaging the full length of the border. I had heard how they were taking food from ranches, stealing horses, and killing people. I knew that my new home was in a vulnerable position for such raids. Most of the ranchmen in our area had moved their families to town for safety at this time. Our neighbors to the south at Glen Springs in the Chisos Mountains had already suffered bloodshed. I knew that I would have to be very careful in whatever I did, yet I was prepared to face all odds. This final acceptance of my life with Roy eased my mind, and I soon drifted into a restful sleep.

It seemed to me that I had hardly lapsed into sleep when Roy, who had slept the whole night through, woke me with a cup of coffee in his hand. "Drink this, then crawl out and get dressed so the boys can come in for their coffee," he said as he moved me off the pallet, tied up the bed, and stashed it away in the corner of the room.

I was in no mood to greet the boys so early in the morning. With coffee in hand and half awake, I left the kitchen and made my way to a rock at the top of the large sand dune that lay just back of the house to sit and drink my coffee in my own silence. The sun was coming up over Stillwell Mountain as I glanced at the wide expanse of country before me. Not a breath of air was stirring, and the peaceful surroundings of early morning calmed my inner thoughts. I was fully prepared for another day as Jona stuck his head out the back door and called to me, "Biscuits are ready!"

Roy in Mexico

ROY STILLWELL was a tall, blue-eyed man respected for his honesty and kindness by those who knew him. Behind his winning smile was enough toughness for him to hold his own in this pioneer country.

He understood the vast land, the people, and the cattle that were peculiar to the Big Bend area. In his life, he wanted a wife, children, a home, and his own ranch. On his ranch, he wanted good cattle and horses. Sometimes I thought he loved his horses above all things or people, including me.

John and Emily Stillwell, Roy's parents, lived in Lagarto, Texas, near Beeville when Roy was born, the seventh of nine children in this family. Roy's family remained in Lagarto for the first seven years of his life. When Roy was two years old, John was given a grant of land in Mexico by the Mexican government. He had up until this time dedicated his services to Maximilian and his wife, Carlotta, during their reign in Mexico and had provided needed medical supplies to their armies during the raging wars of that era. Because of his contributions to the Mexican government and its people, John Stillwell acquired a large piece of land in Mexico, which he hoped to use for raising cattle one day.

In 1884, when Roy was seven years old, John Stillwell decided to move his family to this land in the mountains of Coahuila, Mexico, some twenty-nine miles south of the Rio Grande near the Big Bend country. The country was rough, rugged, and plagued by bandits, but John was strong and wanted to claim his land.

After crossing the Rio Grande and traveling for several days in Mexico, young Roy became too exhausted to complete the trip to the Stillwells' new home. John and Emily stopped at a friendly Indian camp to give Roy a rest. The family was forced to remain in this camp for several days because Roy was making no progress. During this time, the Stillwell family became good friends of these Indians and placed their trust in them completely. In John's hurry to get to his land, the family allowed the Indians to keep Roy in hopes that he would be well cared for and recover his health. John and Emily were concerned that Roy would suffer much more if he continued on with them into unknown territory. They planned to return for him as soon as they had located their property and established their ranch. Roy remained with these Indians for several months before his father returned for him. When living with these Indians, Roy picked up many of their customs and learned many things that helped him later in life. During the time Roy lived with them, he also learned their language, which he never forgot. However, because a major part of his life was spent in Mexico, Spanish was the language that he used until he was about twenty years old, including the Spanish dialects of the Coahuila and Chihuahua Mexicans.

6. John Stillwell, Roy's father

After a short period of time in Mexico, John knew that life under those conditions was too hard on Emily and decided to move her and Roy to Marathon. John packed up his wife and returned to the Indian camp for Roy. On his return trip from Marathon, after settling Emily and Roy there, John found that crossing the Rio Grande could often be difficult. To facilitate his crossing he built a barge that would carry horses, supplies, and travelers across the river and anchored the barge to the bank of the river after each crossing. Soon many others began to use this same barge, a system much easier than swimming or riding horseback. The crossing where the barge was placed became known as Stillwell Crossing, a name still used today.

While in Marathon, Roy attended school. School was of little in-

16

7. Emily Kay Stillwell, Roy's mother

terest to him, and he often found reasons to skip classes. One day Roy and three other boys skipped school and were playing croquet near the railroad depot in the middle of Marathon. While the three boys were playing, Roy said to another boy, "Bet you can't roll that croquet ball down the railroad rail!"

The boy quickly accepted the bet and placed the ball upon the rail. There the ball rolled precariously along the track, balancing as it rolled. The laughing boys followed the ball for some yards when they looked up and saw a hand cart loaded with three men coming toward them. The boys knew what was ahead. As soon as the cart hit the ball it overturned, sending three grown men flying into the air. The three boys mounted their horses and all headed in different directions.

Roy rode his horse south until he reached Persimmon Gap. There he stopped and ate a meal with Mr. and Mrs. Julius Bird, friends of the Stillwells. He told them that he was on his way to see his father, and they accepted that. That day was the end of Roy's schooling and

17

his life in town with his mother. He never was much of a town boy after that.

Roy spent many years on a cattle ranch located in the Piceteria, Fronterieza, and Del Carmen mountains of northern Mexico on the dividing line between the states of Chihuahua and Coahuila. He understood the Mexican people and the raising of Mexican cattle. The Stillwell family members who lived and ranched in Mexico were John; his sons, John, Joe, Will, Roy, and Charlie; and his daughters, Alice and Nellie. While on the ranch in Mexico, Nellie died at an early age and was buried on the Texas side of the Rio Grande. Two older daughters, Lizzie, married to Gus Rountree, and Lola, married to W. S. Brown, lived in Beeville, Texas. Roy's mother Emily spent most of her time in Marathon, where she was more comfortable. The Stillwell boys and Alice operated the huge ranch successfully for several years and made many friends among the Mexican people.

All went well for the family until a man named Cheesman moved into the area where the Stillwells had their holdings. He wanted the Stillwell grant. John Stillwell refused to sell to him, so Cheesman hired the Mexican army to run the Stillwells out of the country. Cheesman had plenty of money and arrived as a "big shot" in Mexico. He aspired to own a cattle empire, and because in Mexico at that time there was no law and order and no courts or justice for the people, he was able to buy the government's army. This army was all-powerful, and their arms and munitions ruled the country with an iron hand. It was common for the army to accept mordida (pay) for favors. The army did just this and acted under his direction and supervision.

The Stillwell family soon recognized their plight and prepared to move their cattle to the Texas side of the Rio Grande. It took three years of fighting to get their cattle to Texas and hold them. They accomplished this enormous task by rounding up small bunches of their cattle at a time and then moving them across the Rio Grande, often in the middle of the night. This was necessary because the Mexican soldiers would not allow any of the Stillwell cattle to cross the Rio Grande; they always found some legal technicality or reason to prevent John from moving his herd to Texas. Their struggle turned out to be a "cat and mouse" movement.

On one particular occasion, Roy, Will, and Alice were hidden in a canyon some twelve miles from the Rio Grande crossing. Thinking that they had eluded the Mexican soldiers and were safe, they built a campfire on which they planned to cook their evening meal.

As they were preparing their meal, a spray of bullets passed through their camp. One bullet knocked a skillet out of Will's hand, and Alice had a bullet driven through her hat, leaving a memorable hole. The group hid in the bushes and watched as the soldiers raided their camp and stole their horses and saddles. The clan gathered together and began walking. In the darkness of the night they managed to make the twelve-mile trip to the Rio Grande and reached safety on the Texas side of the river. They felt they were lucky to have escaped with just the clothes on their backs.

After the Stillwells had been in Texas for a few days, Roy borrowed horses from some of his ranch friends at Marathon. One of Roy's close friends, Punch Roberts, volunteered to go with Roy and Will across the Mexican border and help bring back the confiscated stock. Their plan was partially successful although Punch Roberts later reported that he had never been so scared in all his life. The trio had to sneak up to the Mexican ranch and steal their horses back (they were unable to get their saddles). Upon their return to Texas, Punch Roberts let out an Indian war whoop and blessed the land he had thought he might never see again.

The Rurales (Mexican Federal Border Guards) knew of the Stillwells' problems with the Mexican army and Cheesman; they befriended the Stillwell family and often offered help in their fight to keep their own cattle. Many times during these rough years in Mexico, the people of the Mexican army and the government officials had conflicting ideas. The Stillwells were the only Anglos living in this area of Mexico during this time period, but they were not alone. They had made many Mexican friends, some of them prominent Mexican officials. On one occasion, one of the Rurales, already a trusted friend, told Roy to be at a certain place on the Mexican side of the Rio Grande at a certain time.

Roy asked why; the Rurale answered dogmatically, "You be there and don't be seen!" He then turned and rode away.

Roy followed the man's advice. He approached the designated site cautiously and hid in the brush and waited. Soon he heard cattle moving in from a canyon that formed a bend before it joined the Rio Grande. It was at this bend that Roy was hiding with his rifle ready in his hand. As the cattle rounded the bend, Roy rode out in front of the cattle to turn them toward the Texas side of the river. Just as he began to turn the cattle, three soldiers appeared from behind the herd. Roy heard one of the soldiers shout to another to stop the herd from crossing the river.

At this point, Roy made himself visible to the soldiers and pointed his gun at them. He held the men at gunpoint until all of the cattle were safely across the river and on the Texas side. He then shouted at the men, "Go, and go fast!" They did.

The cattle being moved by the soldiers were, of course, Stillwell cattle that had been stolen by Cheesman and his paid soldiers. Roy drove the cattle to the Dove Mountain and Maravillas area some twenty miles north of the Rio Grande where he was planning to settle. He had begun to believe that the Texas side of the border was a better place to be. The Stillwell family still had their holdings in Mexico, but were beginning to plan a major move to Texas.

In the meantime, W. T. (Billy) Henderson, a young ranchman from San Saba, had driven a herd of horses to Mexico in hopes of finding grazing pastures for his herd. He met the Stillwells at that time, and Henderson made a deal to pasture his horses on the Stillwell land. He decided to stay with the Stillwells and help them with their ranching ventures in Mexico. It was during this time that Alice fell in love with Billy. The two spent many hours together on the ranch and often worked side by side. It was not long before Billy proposed to Alice and they were married. While the threats from Cheesman were becoming more and more frequent, the Henderson couple established a ranch north of Alpine and began to build a herd of cattle from the Stillwell cattle that were being gradually smuggled across the Rio Grande to the Texas side. An unfortunate circumstance took Billy from this ranch for a time, and Roy and his brothers assisted Alice in building up the Henderson Ranch. Billy had been falsely accused of stealing horses in Mexico. Because of the poor communication between the Texas and Mexican governments, Billy was found guilty and forced to serve two years in prison. While Billy was serving his term, the close-knit Stillwell family survived many hard times and suffered many traumas but always kept the family respect for one another. Alice was in constant anticipation of Billy's return and kept the ranch proudly, knowing that he would soon be by her side.

Alice was a fearless woman who was highly respected in Texas and Mexico for her ability to ranch, work cattle, and ride horseback as well as any man. She took her troubles into her own hands and never backed down from any problems. She rode beside the men, worked as hard as they did, and produced quality work that any cowboy would acknowledge as "the best."

During one confrontation with the Mexican army that took place before Billy was sent to prison, a soldier stole Billy's favorite gun. When Alice learned that the gun was gone, without offering any explanation to her husband or brothers she saddled her pony and rode alone over many rough miles in search of the soldiers' camp. After a long ride, she located their campsite and rode right into the camp, jumped from her horse at the entrance to their tent, threw open the flap, and pointed her gun at the men inside. She held them at gunpoint while she recovered her husband's gun from one of the soldiers. She then quickly turned, mounted her pony, and left at a run.

Several of the soldiers went after Alice, and a race for the border was on. Alice approached a corral that held a herd of horses and decided to attempt to outsmart the soldiers. She was far enough ahead of the soldiers and was such a good horsewoman that she was able to enter the corral quietly. Being a small-framed woman who rode a diminutive pony, she could hide among the horses' massive bodies. As she quietly nestled among them, she never moved a muscle. The soldiers rushed past the corral, not seeing her at all. As the soldiers faded from sight, she mounted her pony and headed in the opposite direction from the Rio Grande border toward Musquiz, where she found lodging. A few days went by, and Alice returned to Texas and gave her husband his gun, much to his surprise. This is just one of the incidents that gained her the respect of anyone who had ever questioned her ability to be equal to any man. From that time on, most stood in awe of this tiny West Texas woman.

Shortly after this incident and the imprisonment of Billy, Roy and the rest of the Stillwell family decided that the ruthlessness of so many of the Mexican people along the Rio Grande was reason enough to look toward Texas soil. Roy believed that so little law and order existed in Mexico that living there would soon be disastrous for anyone who was not a Mexican. The Stillwells therefore gave up their holdings in Mexico but kept their longtime Mexican friends on the "other side."

Pants, Boots, and Spurs

ALTHOUGH Roy had explained to me about the Stillwell ranching operation in Mexico, it was hard for me to visualize the family life there and the hardships they endured. I could readily see Roy's love for and loyalty to his brothers and sisters, especially Alice, who was his idol and the person who influenced his life the most.

Alice was responsible for teaching Roy to respect women. Her example of being a lady in the midst of the toughest, most ruthless men was uppermost in Roy's mind as he talked of her life. When she was riding and working cattle, she dressed in men's clothing, worked like a man, and never shirked her duty.

However, when Alice went to town to buy supplies or tend to duties in town, she always donned a skirt and appeared as neat and womanly as any other lady during this time. She was the perfect lady when need be and the perfect ranchwoman when necessary. I loved to hear Roy talk of her, and I would often catch myself wondering if I could follow in Alice's footsteps. Then, there would be times when I would tell myself, "No! I can only be me and go my own way the best I can. I'm living in Texas now and not in Mexico." But I did know that I could learn from her experiences.

I thought that I was well prepared for horseback riding and doing light work around the place; however, nothing happened the way I dreamed it would. In growing up, I had passed the sidesaddle era and in that year, 1918, ladies were permitted to ride dressed in a long flowing divided skirt. I had brought along such a riding skirt when Roy and I first came to the ranch, and I thought I looked really nice with it on. It was made of heavy khaki material with a flap of material across the front so that no division in the skirt would show. I felt that I was really prepared for a day's ride as I walked from the house to where the men were waiting for me the first time I planned to ride with the men. Not so! When Roy gave me a startled look and asked if I had some pants, I knew something was wrong.

I said, "This is what I ride in!"

"Hell, you can't ride in that thing. There's not a horse in this part of the country that will let a thing like that on it," said Roy as he glared at my beautiful riding skirt. "You'll have to have some pants."

I knew that I could not get into any of Roy's pants; he was tall, slender, and had positively no hips. I was tall for a woman but certainly had full hips. I told Roy that my mother would have to make some kind of pants for me to use when riding, because I knew that the stores did not carry pants for women. The only problem was that I would have to go to Alpine.

Roy got down off his horse, shoved the men off to work, stalked into the house with me following closely behind, and told me to get ready to go to town.

So, off to Alpine and Mama we went. When I told Mama what we had come to town for, she was horrified. "Roy, you don't mean to let your wife wear pants in front of all those cowboys, do you? They will lose respect for her," moaned my mother who had always been

8. Hallie (far right) in her riding gear

a fine protected and sheltered lady of southern breeding. In her wildest imagination, she could not vision her daughter riding off in men's pants to goodness knows where, and goodness knows with whom.

Roy told her, "It's for her protection. You know we can't leave her at home alone. With Pancho Villa and God only knows who else roaming around the country, she'll have to ride with us and she'll have to wear pants; as far as respect, that's up to her!"

Mama gathered up all her courage, blinked her eyes, shook her head, and headed toward the bedroom. I was not sure what to expect.

Mama, bless her sweet soul, was a good seamstress. She had made clothes for me all my life. Without a pattern of any kind, she designed and made a pair of pants the likes of which no one had ever seen before or afterward. As soon as she had finished them, we bundled them up without me trying them on and headed back to the ranch. We were in a hurry to be off, and I knew that Mama had made enough clothing for me that fitting would be no problem. I felt that I was well prepared then and could mount any of Roy's horses because I was an experienced rider and loved horses. I arrived at the ranch that evening feeling very confident about myself as a ranchman's wife. I was ready for anything.

The next morning I dressed for the day in my new riding pants.

23

Not having a mirror, I could not see how I looked. I knew that something was not right, but I could not figure out the problem. The pants were gathered in at the waist band and hung very full down to the knees. Here the stride of the pants hung low and full. Below the knees, these pants buttoned tightly down the sides of each leg all the way to my ankles. I thought they looked really neat, but they felt strange – not as strange, though, as the looks on Roy and the boys' faces as I approached the horse that they were holding for me. Lee held the reins, and Roy stood by to help me mount as Tuff stood idly by and observed. I had never been assisted in getting on a horse before, and I wondered about all the attention being paid me. With one hand on the saddle horn and my foot in the stirrup, I gave myself a boost. Instead of landing in the saddle upright, I hung the stride of those wonderful pants firmly on the back of the saddle. I could not move. I could not get up or down.

Those well-made pants would not give or rip. The beautiful buttons down the sides had no resilience. I could not get myself off the high perch on which I had placed myself. Roy tried to help me as Lee kept his tight hold onto the horse's reins. The horse humped his back, jumped from side to side, and attempted in every way to rid himself of me. He wanted no part of the mess I had put us both in. It was certainly a toss-up as to who was most frightened, me or the horse. Tuff finally got into the act and by pushing me one way and Roy pulling the other, they were able to free me from my precarious position on the trembling horse.

Jona, who was still asleep, heard the commotion and came to see what the trouble might be. After being told about the riding pants tragedy, he said that he had a pair of pants that I might be able to wear. Roy brought them to me. I went into the house, put them on, pulled on my boots, took one of Roy's hats off the wall, and with my head held high I walked out of the house and up to the horse they were still holding for me. I gathered up the reins, mounted, and rode off for the day with three silent men following closely behind.

As I rode off, I thought of my mother and the horror that she would experience if she could have seen me in that man's pants. I knew that she only wanted the best for me, but I also knew that I must adapt to my new environment if I was going to remain on the ranch. To this day, I do not know what became of the pants my mother had made for me, but I never mentioned them to her. They were an experience that I and those men never forgot but never spoke of again.

I soon learned that the dress that I was expected to wear was much different from that of a "town lady." Roy bought me a pair of boots that would help protect my legs, allow me to ride through cacti and rough country, and give me the needed support necessary for riding in the saddle all day. Comfort and protection soon became more important in my dress than looks or what others thought.

Papa very proudly had given me his favorite pair of spurs, which I used as long as I rode horses on the Stillwell Ranch. They were very special to me because I knew that secretly Papa, although he never voiced it to anyone, was extremely proud of me for my ability to adjust to ranch life and my determination to work and ride as well as any man. Papa himself had once been a ranchman in his earlier days. He and I both knew how Mama felt about my being a lady and presenting myself in a proper manner at all times. Papa's feelings were just something I knew in my heart.

Although I wore men's pants, I soon found that I needed more protection for my legs and my boots. As I rode, I would often get catclaw or cactus needles stuck in my legs, and I realized that the rough country brush was ruining my boots. I needed more. I somehow appropriated an old pair of chaps from Tuff. Those chaps saved me much pain and discomfort and I was very glad to have them.

I discovered that the intense heat, sandy winds, and dusty rides were becoming a burden to my soft and delicate skin, which my mother had taught me at an early age to keep healthy. I began to wear long-sleeved shirts, high necks, and gloves whenever we were riding or working cattle. Roy felt that the gloves were a hindrance but I had always worn gloves, even before I met him, and I was not going to give them up. He would frequently tell me whenever I fumbled or botched a job that I should get rid of the gloves and I would be able to maneuver better. I would always quickly reply, "If I take off these gloves, I will not be able to do anything right." My gloves were made of soft deerskin and were almost a part of my body.

I even powdered my face and put on lipstick before I left the house for a day's work. During one of my earlier preparations for a day's work, Roy stood in the doorway as I was putting on my powder and lipstick. I knew he was going to say something, and he did.

"Do you think those cows will notice whether you have lipstick on or not?"

I continued my ritual and explained to Roy that what I was doing was just as much protection for my skin as my boots and chaps were for my legs. He never asked again but I knew that he thought my makeup procedures just wasted important time.

Being reared during a time when ladies were supposed to have delicate white skin, Mama had always made me wear a bonnet whenever I went outside. If I started out the door without my bonnet I could count on hearing Mama ask, "Daughter, where are your bonnet and gloves?"

So, when I first stepped out to ride with Roy, I was clad in my favorite bonnet. Needless to say, Roy did not approve. He promptly told me to remove the bonnet and don a hat. He said I could not see anything with that bonnet on. I reluctantly gave up my bonnet for one of Roy's felt Stetsons.

I soon found that my dress was certainly not typical of a lady or schoolteacher but learned the great importance of it. I grew to depend on my attire as much as I depended on a good saddle and horse. I learned a great deal as each day passed, and I began to feel more and more a part of the ranch.

Cowboys

WHEN Roy and his family successfully got their cattle out of Mexico and closed a deal with Cheesman, Roy and his brothers and sister developed their own individual spreads. As Roy chose his land and built his ranch, he created a new family that consisted of those who worked for and with him. Since there was no woman on his ranch, the men soon became as close-knit as any family. Besides being working partners on the ranch, they depended on one another for company as well.

Lee Walker, a native of Brewster County, was a good hand with cows, horses, and general ranchwork. Lee did not have the advantages of schooling as he grew up on the open ranges. All he knew was from his life's experiences, which were limited to mostly ranch work. Roy liked Lee because he was honest, trustworthy, and willing to spend months on end alone in the country. As far as I know Lee never looked at a woman and was too shy to speak to one. Lee could track a panther over slick rocks, set a trap for coyotes, and keep track of the movements of cattle and horses. Lee looked to Roy for his livelihood and well-being. It is no wonder he took a dim view of a woman's being brought into camp.

Eschol Hatch, known through the neighborhood and Marathon as Tuff, was small, and hardly tall enough to reach the horn of his saddle on a small pony. Tuff had come to work for Roy when he was twelve years old and stayed with him until he was drafted into the army during World War I. Roy always said that Tuff would not lie, even if it took the hide off his body, and Roy said that he could always depend on Tuff to do as he was told.

Jona Akard, who could ride the fiercest bronc and never scratch leather, was not too dependable. He was from a fine family. He had brothers who were professional men, and even Jona had a good education. However, he had some sort of sleeping sickness that was rare in those days. Doctors had been consulted by his family in hopes that Jona's sickness could be cured, but to no avail. Jona, feeling that he did not belong with his real family, turned from them and drifted west by following the cowboy trail. He had been with Roy for several years when I came to the ranch. Whatever his troubles, Jona was a kind and patient man. He taught me many things about working cattle that Roy would not take time to teach me.

During one of my first attempts to help the men work cattle, I was struggling with a calf I was trying to tie down, and Jona came to my rescue. He said, "You're doing it all backwards; just take the tie rope in your left hand, take the feet of the calf in your right hand, then wrap them up just like this." He showed me how to take advantage of a calf while throwing him and acting at the right moment when all four feet were off the ground – a time of less than one second. He also taught me how to hold a calf down by securing the front leg and just how and where to be positioned in order to protect myself from dangerous kicks. Thanks to Jona, I was soon an expert at throwing and tying down almost any size calf. Because of Jona and his understanding, I began to feel that I was on my way to becoming a real help on the ranch.

Jona was good help always for the first few days of cow work. After that we expected him to spend most of his time in camp asleep. He would be good about having food ready when we all came in tired and hungry and I have always thought that he made the best biscuits in the world.

Besides the cowboy family, Roy also worked "wet" Mexicans, men who crossed the Rio Grande illegally from Mexico looking for work. These men were used to break broncs, dig postholes, and perform the manual labor around the ranch. They usually stayed long enough to get enough money to take back to Mexico to feed their families for a month or so. Occasionally an older Mexican man would show up looking for work because he had no family and would stay much longer, but for the most part, the Mexican workers were passing through just looking for temporary work. These men came and went much like the changing weather in West Texas. They were never a part of Roy's ranch family but were an integral part of the workings of the ranch.

Roy prepared me to deal with these Mexican men looking for work. He told me never to allow any of these men in our yard without an invitation. Roy's instructions were very clear. "Hallie, never allow one of these men past the front gate. If one comes through the gate, shoot him!"

I was at first astonished at his remark. "You mean you want me to shoot him just like that?"

"Yes, if he gets past the gate it will be too late. All these men who are looking for work know to wait at the gate for an invitation. Anyone who does not know this is not looking for work but for something more."

I felt somewhat uncomfortable about this but I knew that I had to protect myself and the ranch. As I shuddered, Roy reminded me, "There is a loaded gun in every corner of the house. If you need to use one, get the closest one and make the first shot count. Remember, never shoot to scare but shoot to kill!"

From that day on I stayed prepared for any man who walked up to our gate. I never had to shoot at anyone but I faced many men at our gate. Fortunately the Stillwell Ranch had been established as a good place to work and this word was passed throughout the border area. Most Mexicans knew of Roy's reputation and respected him. Many Mexican men worked for us, and we never turned one away if he was hungry or thirsty. After a few months on the ranch, I began to relax and accept the Mexican men, the ranch hands, and my new way of life. In a short time, I was a part of the family.

One winter Roy put Lee and Jona together at the Dove Mountain ranch to look after the cattle while Roy and I stayed at headquarters. After a couple of months, Roy went to check on them, taking a load of groceries for the men and a load of salt for the cows. Jona took Roy to one side and told him that he thought that something was wrong with Lee. He told Roy that Lee had strange ideas and that he was getting tired of listening to Lee babble all the time.

Roy assured Jona that Lee was harmless and told him not to pay any attention to Lee's talk. Before the day was over, Lee took Roy aside by a water tank and whispered to him, "Look Roy, Jona says such funny things. I think something is wrong with him." Roy then had to assure *Lee* that nothing was wrong with *Jona*. He told Lee that they would soon be coming back to headquarters for the rest of the winter. This seemed to satisfy Lee for the moment.

When Roy told me about the conflict between the two men, we decided that they had been together too long on the lonely ranch. There had been no outsiders for them to talk with. In those days, there were no radios, televisions, or newspapers. With just the two of them together, there is no wonder that there was tension between them.

Another time, Jona and Lee were at another camp together. One morning before sunup, they were squatted down by the campfire drinking coffee. Jona had a full cup and had started to take his first sip when he fell asleep. This caused him to tilt his cup, which splashed hot coffee all over his own leg. He jerked his head upright quickly and said to Lee, "Think you're damn smart, don't you?"

Lee just looked at Jona, shrugged his shoulders, and said, "Jona, you know damn well I didn't do that!"

I have seen Jona drop off to sleep while riding a bronc. The bronc would brush against a sticker bush or Spanish dagger, causing pain to Jona's legs or arms. This would wake him and he would be furious at the bronc. Then he would spur him and make him pitch even more than he had before. In all these lapses of sleep, Jona was never thrown. No one understood his illness, but everyone who knew him loved and admired him in spite of it. And, even though Jona and Lee had experienced difficult times together, they remained constant and good friends for as long as they were on our ranch.

There were times when these workmen would get terribly frustrated with Roy, but they seldom complained. Roy, being a quiet man who never really had much to say, would often depend on the workmen to know what to do without being told. I have since met and known many ranchwomen in the West Texas area who have told me that their husbands often act in this same manner. For cowboys, the life of a ranchman is nothing to brag about, their problems are nothing to discuss with other people, and their business is very confidential. Because of this typical attitude of most of the ranchmen in the West Texas area, few have much to say, and most expect others to know what they are thinking at all times. Roy was certainly this type of person. This made life on our ranch somewhat complicated at times.

Roy never told the men what to do or where to go. This frustration led the men to think of something that would show Roy just how difficult life could be working on the ranch without really being told what was expected. They came up with a scheme to gauge just how far Roy would go without giving a command. This effort was an attempt to get even with what I called Roy's "silent spells." These men saddled up one morning ready to ride and waited for their directions. Roy saddled up and rode off. The men just remained doggedly behind as Roy rode out into the pasture and never looked back. The men, determined to make their points, sat at the ranch house all morning long, but Roy never returned to give them their orders. Their wait became an extremely nervous and frustrating one.

When noon came, the men left their spots and walked quietly into the house for lunch. They were a tired-looking bunch with drooping heads. Jona whispered to me that he and the men really did not mean any harm; they just wanted to show Roy the importance of knowing what to do. Jona was really worried about Roy's response. It was then obvious that the men's plan had not worked and Roy was not going to play their game.

The men had not been in the house long when Roy came in for lunch. They all ate very quietly and the three anxious men waited for Roy's reaction. When the group had finished eating, Roy got up, put on his hat, turned to the men, and said, "C'mon boys!" The men jumped up and followed like hungry puppies after their mother.

Lee told me later that he was never so glad to hear anybody say anything to him in his whole life. This stunt did not open Roy up any more, but I do believe that they all learned a good lesson that day.

Even though these men had their own individual problems, they were all good and faithful to Roy. They worked well together, understood one another most of the time, and respected one another for their expertise in the ranching business. Roy could not have been such a successful ranchman without these hard-working, trustworthy men to help him. They were his "ranch family."

Dove Mountain

IN 1906, Roy homesteaded and settled a ranch about twenty miles from the border and near the mouth of the Maravillas Creek where it meets the Rio Grande. A year after he established this ranch he called Dove Mountain, he also began ranching various open ranges. His favorite was where the Stillwell Ranch is today. In 1914, Roy purchased approximately fifteen sections near the Maravillas Creek from Hubert Wizzell, an Englishman. There Roy built his headquarters and used this place as home.

He had worked hard to create a good ranch for his cattle, and by the time we had married in 1918, Dove Mountain had become an important part of Roy's ranching business. He had built two small buildings; two water tanks, one on the north side and one at the home-site; and corrals to accommodate his stock. There were no fences during that time, and Roy's cattle grazed the open ranges. I soon learned that a trip to the Dove Mountain place meant hard work. I knew that the cattle at Dove Mountain were spread over open ranges and it would take days to work them. When we had worked the cattle there we were always exhausted and ready to return to headquarters.

"Better round up your duds, we've got to go work Dove Mountain," said Roy one morning shortly after we were settled on the ranch.

"When? How long will we be gone?" I asked.

"We've got to shoe the horses and fix up the chuck wagon, should get off in a couple of days, probably be over there a couple of weeks if we have good luck. You better start rounding up a little grub."

Activity started in right after those words. Lee rode off and brought in the remuda (saddle horses used for cow work), and the shoeing of horses started. I couldn't keep my mind on that grub box very well for my watching the men in the pens with the horses. Their language was rather strong, and I wondered why they bothered to put shoes on the horses when it seemed to be such an ordeal for all concerned. Most of the horses were not too bad, but one named Orb was spoiled and obviously didn't want to be shod. Roy had to tie him down, all four feet (this is called "hog-tied"), to tack the shoes on his hooves. Orb was a horse that seemed to have a natural grudge against mankind, and he never failed to get a kick or bite at Roy whenever he got a chance. Lee was afraid even to get in the pen with this horse, but Roy thought that he was an excellent cow horse, and he depended on this horse when he needed to cover lots of country. Roy could do more work on Orb than he could on any other two of his horses together.

We finally got all the horses shod, and the chuck wagon packed with the chuck box, bedrolls, branding irons, ropes, and other odds and ends that would be needed for the works. Roy decided that he and I would drive the wagon and let Lee and Tuff take the remuda over. It was ten miles and over two mountains from our ranch head-quarters to the Dove Mountain ranch. The road we had to travel was just an unglorified cow trail. Roy had hitched two wild mules to our wagon, and he and I mounted ourselves high up in the spring seat. Just as I relaxed in the wagon seat, Roy asked if I had my spurs on.

"What on earth for?" I asked.

"You'll need them if you're going to ride in this wagon with these two mules pulling." Roy released the brake and those mules bolted like they had been shot from a torpedo. I hung on tightly to the seat, and a wilder ride I have never had. The little mules calmed quite a bit after we climbed the first mountain, but as we started down the canyon, one wheel ran over a huge boulder and Roy lost his balance. He fell down onto the doubletree. He was so funny looking with his long legs dragging under the mules' hind heels that I could not help but laugh. Well, that was the worst thing I could have done. As soon as Roy could get his balance, he scrambled back up to the seat. He was highly insulted and asked me incredulously, "How can you laugh? These mules could have stampeded and dragged me to death!"

I rode silently after that incident. Roy and I survived the trip and got to the Dove Mountain ranch house all safe and sound. I vowed then that I didn't want any more chuck wagon rides. That was to be my last. I either went horseback or, in later years, I rode in the truck.

As we rode up to the Dove Mountain place, I felt that I had indeed come to the jumping-off place at the end of the world. I somehow knew that I would never be the same again. I found out quickly that I was to live like a man, work like a man, and act like a man, and I was not so sure I was not a man when it was all over. The good Lord did give me a mind that could not be governed by a man, and I remained a woman. I feel sure at times now that this one fact caused me lots of grief, but also lots of happiness.

We all pitched in to make our camp comfortable. While Roy and I unloaded the wagon, Tuff tended to the remuda and Lee gathered some firewood. I thought that Lee would use the wagon to haul in some wood, but he just rode off on his horse. After a while, he came back dragging a big bundle of wood wrapped up with his rope and tied to the saddle horn. His horse was snorting and prancing because he didn't like the racket that the bundle behind him was making. I felt sorry for the pony but soon learned that that type of thing was just part of the training for a cow pony. After Lee cut a few sticks for firewood, he built a big fire in the stove, and then went to the tank and brought up two big buckets of water and put them on the stove to boil.

"Well, looks like we're going to clean up the place good, "I thought to myself.

When the water got boiling hot, Lee took one bucket after the other and started pouring the hot water in the cracks of the floor. I immediately thought that that was a crazy way to clean a floor. It was evident that the floor needed a good scrubbing but most of the water was just pouring through the planks. I had learned to be slow about questioning the cowboys, but when I could stand it no longer I asked, "Lee, why pour that hot water through the cracks in the floor? You can't clean a floor that way!"

"Hell, I'm not going to clean the floor, got to get the rattlesnakes and skunks out from under this house if we intend to stay here. I'm not going to make down my bedroll until every stinking one is run out."

I was glad that Roy and I had a bedstead and springs to put our bedroll on, for I knew that Roy would not take the pains to pour that much hot water through the cracks in the room where we were going to bed down.

Our camp house didn't seem so bad after we had stayed a few days. In fact, it was rather neat in the kitchen after our meals were cooked, and we had tied all the food up on the rafters in flour sacks to keep the rats and skunks from getting into them. We had also put the tin cups and plates and knives and forks on the top of the stove to dry and be kept clean.

We were camped there for the purpose of working our cattle, not housekeeping, so all hands turned to the work in earnest. Every morning at early dawn, while the ice was still hard in the troughs, we saddled up and started out. The horses were fresh and frisky and sometimes even the gentlest and best horse humped and pitched a few jumps before he could get going. I think I often felt the same as those horses.

The first day of work at Dove Mountain was rather successful. We did find one bull that was poor and needed feeding, so Roy decided that I should be the one to ride back to headquarters and get a sack of cake in hopes that this would save the bull. The bull looked pretty bad, and I felt sorry for him. Roy saddled up the night horse for me to ride. His name was Old Dun. When I got ready to leave, Roy said, "Better lope all the way over there – ten miles is a long way, and you will have to come back slowly because you'll be carrying the cake." Those were all the instructions that I received before I left.

I loped all the way over to headquarters. I had to drag the sack of cake out of the barn. Roy had told me to load this sack weighing one hundred pounds onto my horse. There was no way I could get the sack loaded onto my horse, and there was not a living soul at the ranch to help me. I decided to divide the cake into two sacks. I tried to put the two sacks on Old Dun but he refused. He shied and snorted at those sacks, and I could not hold him and lift the sacks at the same time. I kept thinking that Roy had sent me for this cake and I must deliver or else. I was really in a fix and getting madder and madder all the time. I had to find a way to load the cake and get going. It was getting late and I needed to get back to Dove Mountain.

I looked over at the corral fence and came up with an idea. I placed the two sacks on the fence, mounted Old Dun, and attempted to ride up next to the fence. I anticipated getting one sack of cake in front of me and one behind. I knew if I could slip up next to the fence, I could get this done. But Old Dun would have none of this. I could get almost there, then he would start backing away and start prancing. I was beginning to lose my patience. I then chose to act like the cowboys to see how that would work. I jerked up the reins, spurred Old Dun as hard as I could and let out an oath in my loudest voice. I hit him over the head with my quirt and spurred him once again toward the fence. He obeyed and stood still as I loaded both sacks of cake and tied them onto the saddle. I started back in a high trot to Dove Mountain. It was very late when I got there and Roy, Lee, and Tuff had begun to worry. Roy didn't say much about me being late for he could see that I was tired and cross.

When Lee had a chance, he whispered to me, "I don't know why Roy put you on Old Dun, he is the worst horse on this ranch. We never use him except for a night horse. I knew you would catch hell." (A night horse is a horse kept in a corral and used to retrieve the remuda each morning – usually an old and worthless horse.)

I did not tell Lee, but secretly I think that Roy made me ride Old Dun because I had laughed at him when he fell out of the wagon onto the doubletree. Roy always had a way of getting back at me.

Roy had good saddle horses and he always kept them fat. It was against his principles to ride a poor horse or an old one. But fat young horses on cold brisk mornings had to be handled with ease. During this work, each of us had three mounts and I did not have to ride Old Dun the night horse any more. One of my mounts was named Grace. He was a small grey pony that had been broken and trained for a polo pony, but the man who owned him could not manage him. Roy decided to purchase him and make a cow pony out of him. The first time Roy put me on him he told me to mount very quickly, and said to me, "Don't hive any gnats"– meaning don't daydream –"or you'll land behind the saddle." I always felt that Roy was reading my "death sentence" when he gave me one of his warnings. "And another thing," Roy said, "if you are off in the country by yourself and see that you are going to have to get off that horse, get him up in a rocky place, or you will never get back on him. Now, don't be afraid, but use your head and don't get left afoot away off in those hills and canyons for we are not going to have time to be hunting you."

Well, I rode Grace. I never did land behind the saddle, and every time I got off him I picked a nice rocky hill. I did just as I was told and I did not get left in the canyons. I loved to ride Grace and we were getting along just fine. I thought I was really fixed up for that cow work. But just about the time Grace and I accepted one another, Roy caught a fresh mount for me, and I had to get all acquainted with another horse. Streak was a big bay horse with a blazed face. He stood very still for me to mount, and I could take my time about getting on him. I could get off him on any good smooth flat ground and get on him again with no trouble. But, boy when he got after a cow! It took all I had just to stay on that horse. My third horse was Montereye, one that was supposed to be safe enough for a woman to ride. No one told me about that horse. Everyone just took it for granted that I would be able to ride him. I had to learn to handle him all by myself, a way I believe all "greenhorns" should learn. This, of course, was Roy's way.

One day I was left at camp alone; the boys had an unusually long and hard ride to make, and Roy thought that I had better stay at camp and rest for awhile. After they had been gone for a few hours, I got lonesome and restless. I decided to go hunting. I went to the corral, caught Montereye, saddled him up, got the gun and placed it in the saddle scabbard just as I had seen Roy do, and headed for the nearest bluffs. To get there, I had to "let down" a wire fence that was used as a crossing. I had to dismount, tie down the wire, lead my horse across the wire, and reattach the wire to the fence. I got off when I came to the fence and tied the wire down to the bottom of the post. I then took Montereye by the bridle reins and led him gently over the fence without a bit of trouble. I continued on but found no deer or game to shoot. I returned to camp just as I had come.

When Roy and the boys came in, of course, Roy saw that I had been off some place. When we sat down to supper, he said, "Where did you go today?"

"Hunting," I answered.

"What did you ride?"

"Montereye," I replied.

"Don't you know that you can't carry a gun on that fool horse?" he exclaimed.

"Well, I did just that!"

"Where did you go?"

"Under the bluff," I responded.

"Hell, don't you know that you can't get that horse over a fence? Why, he's a fool about wire!" roared Roy. Then, very calmly, Roy looked at me and asked, "See anything to shoot at?"

"Nope!"

"It's a damn good thing you didn't or you would have probably tried to carry an animal back on that fool horse, and you can't do that either."

I just looked at Roy.

"If that doesn't beat all!" remarked Lee. "That horse wouldn't let me do any of the things she did today! Guess what you don't know is sometimes best."

Tuff said that he guessed they had better not leave me alone anymore, or I would be putting shoes on Old Orb.

I made many more mistakes that I always had to pay for, but the men and Roy guided me and helped me become a good ranchwoman. I learned many things on my own and many things from the men, and I have never regretted any moment that I spent on the ranch. I may have been a "greenhorn" when I married Roy, but in time I began to feel that I had earned my spurs just as any man had.

Learning the Hard Way

THE cow work at Dove Mountain was strenuous and difficult because of the open country, high mountains, and deep canyons. The one makeshift small pasture would not hold more than the saddle horses and a few cattle. Surface water tanks were few and far between. I soon realized that the going would be hard not only on the saddle horses but for all concerned. Slick rocks, cacti, boulders, and desert brush hindered any clean sweep of cattle to be gathered and held for the later movement. A set of holding pens was by far the best improvement of the ranch besides the huge dirt water tank that held water all year long – at least, it always held from one good rain to another. Our neighbors always said that when Stillwell's Dove Mountain tank was about to go dry, a good rain would soon come.

On our last day's work, with most of the cattle gathered, Roy said that we would make one more try at finding certain cattle that had been missed. He directed each cowboy to a specific area. In the meantime, some of our neighbors had sent over their stray men (cowboys who help other ranchers during a roundup and gather any cattle that belong to their bosses). We were glad to have the help as our herd was larger than expected and a lot of hands would be needed to hold them. After the cowboys had been sent to their designated areas, Roy told me to "go over yonder," making a wide sweep with his hand. "Take that draw over there and follow it until you come to a *rincon* [a small valley surrounded by small mountains], then take up the right-hand canyon and top out on a rocky hill, then take down the draw on your left and pick up anything you see." These were my directions from my husband and boss of the outfit.

I took off, hardly knowing where I was going or where I would land. I went to the end of the draw, which came to a broad end with mountains all around, so I supposed that must be the *rincon* he had mentioned. I had never heard of a *rincon* and was not sure whether it was a ditch, a hill, a mound, or a caliche pit, but I thought that surely the place I was was where he meant for me to be. I noticed that the only way out was the canyon to the right. This canyon I followed, not knowing what I would come to next. I rode all day long looking for lost cattle and all I could find were tracks. I saw enough cattle tracks that I felt I should find something, but I didn't. After my long ride and the sun sinking in the west, I noticed what I thought was the hill Roy had told me about.

As I got closer I realized that it *was* the right hill, and I could see on farther down. Roy was driving a few cows toward the north tank. I sure was glad to see that someone was in the country because I was thoroughly lost, not knowing where I had been or how I got there. I think my horse, Streak, helped me and took me where I was supposed to go. I really do believe that my horse understood Roy's directions better than I did. At least, Streak had been in those parts before.

I was so happy and relieved when I caught up with Roy. I was feeling so safe once again that I did not notice the frown on his face. He started in questioning me right away.

"Did you see any cattle?"

"No," I said.

"Did you see any tracks?"

"Yes, I saw some tracks."

"How many in the bunch?"

"A lot."

"Were there any bulls?"

"I don't know."

"Any baby calves?"

"Heck, I don't know, I don't know a thing about tracks!" I answered in frustration.

By that time, I was nearly in tears. I felt that I had let Roy down, and I felt that I was a complete failure. I began to wish that I could go back to where I had come from or that I could crawl into a hole. I was tired, dirty, and hungry. I felt foolish for not being able to read the tracks, and I really felt alone and out of place. I worked myself up to the boiling point and felt that I had 'flubbed the dub.'" At that point, Roy and I met with the other men and all of us returned to camp in complete silence.

Soon after the evening meal, as I was sitting on a rock, looking into the far-away beautiful mountains in Mexico and enjoying the lovely evening shadows so typical of West Texas at dusk, my emotions were calmed and I felt peace and happiness. I thought to myself that I should not let one failure disturb me. Jona could tell that I had been troubled, and he came over and sat down by me hoping to find out why I had such red, tear-stained eyes.

I told Jona about the cow tracks and my failure to read them. Jona very patiently explained to me that bulls made big heavy tracks, calves made small light ones, and cows' tracks were usually weighted somewhere between the two. He said that if I paid close attention, I would soon know whether a bunch of cattle were moving toward or away from water, in what direction they were traveling, whether they were going to graze, and even how many cattle were in a bunch by the tracks left behind. After this lesson about tracks, I felt better and I knew that I had one friend in camp, Jona. After some time, I left my peaceful spot and returned to the campfire.

As the glow of light faded into darkness, I crept into the bedroll I shared with Roy, hoping to rest my tired bones. Roy sat with the men who were talking over the events of the day and discussing the subject of the lost cattle. I lay in our bedroll thinking that I had failed and wondered whether those cow tracks that I had seen were those of the missing cattle. I realized that I did not even know in which direction they had gone. I felt that I had not been any help that day.

I was about to fall asleep when Roy came to bed. As he readied himself for bed, he was whistling, a sign that he was in good spirits. I knew then that he regretted his cold actions toward me earlier in the day.

"Hon," Roy said, "I feel sure those cows we missed have been driven to El Otra Lado." (He was referring to "the other side," or Mexico.)

"I suspect that they've been gone for several days because I noticed a strange horse track down in Dove Mountain Creek. The winds and dust made tracking difficult. I'll send Lee down to the mouth of the Maravillas to take a look while we take the herd on to headquarters. I think the tracks that you saw were old and dim – no wonder you couldn't tell about them. Let's go to sleep now; it'll be a long day tomorrow getting those cattle all the way home."

No truer words were ever spoken. It was definitely a hard day. All hands were up at the crack of dawn; the horses were saddled and the cowboys ready to ride. I was mounted on Grace, who humped up a bit due to the early morning cold, and I thought for a while that I would be spilled, especially when we tore around through ditches and thick brush trying to get the cattle away from the tank of water and on the way to headquarters.

One old cow in particular did not want to leave, and I took it upon myself to see that she did. After a hard chase, I finally got her back into the herd, but not for long. She bolted out from the herd, and no one paid any attention to her. I could see that she would get away, so I took in after her and put her back with the herd. All day long this crazy old cow kept trying to go back to the water tank and would not go along with the herd of cattle.

As we drove the herd over mountains and canyons covered with slick rocks, through sotol plants and all kinds of thick brush and Spanish daggers, I chased that one old ornery cow. Feeling worried and tired and aggravated that no one else seemed concerned, I wondered if my horse, Grace, would hold out long enough to get to headquarters. I knew he was getting sore from all the sticker brush and sharp rocks. I was getting sore from being bounced over that rough country making extra runs to keep that cow in the herd.

Finally, after a long day, the herd was being driven into the holding pasture at headquarters. As everyone began to feel a big relief that the day's work was about the end, the old cow made one more dash out of the herd. I started after her as I had been doing all day and I heard Roy yell loudly and clearly, "Let her go, she's not our cow, didn't want her in the first place!"

I let the cow go, watched as she headed for the tank, and lowered my head as Grace limped toward the group of men. Once again I rode silently to the house.

My humiliation, sore muscles, and tired body were no worse than my horse's. As I unsaddled Grace, I leaned up against his neck and whispered to him, "Boy, we've played hell all day." I then dragged my aching body to the house.

We ate our supper in complete silence; the men were all tired and we all knew how long the day had been. I was not about to break the silence and expose my ignorance. While the men washed up the supper dishes, I went to the dune in back of the kitchen to watch the ever-changing colors on the mountain bluffs as sundown and dusk approached. There I could calm my weary soul and reflect on the days of the Dove Mountain cow work and the mistakes I had made and the humiliation I had endured.

Jona, noticing my retreat and understanding my feelings, came out and sat down beside me on the sand pile and opened up a conversation. "It's been a hard day, hasn't it?"

"Yes," I said. "Why did Roy let me chase that cow all day when he didn't want her?"

"She didn't have Roy's brand, not even the right earmark," explained Jona. "Didn't you notice that her bag was full of milk? Her baby calf was left at the water tank and the cow was trying to go back to it. You need to notice all these things around a herd of cattle. Roy was only trying to make sure you're aware of things that you're going to have to know."

As always, Jona's words to me were soothing to my soul, and I soon felt much better. Once again I was so thankful that I had Jona around to help me become a better ranchwoman.

After this lesson I recovered and was ready once again to work with Roy and the men. It did not take long after we had the Dove Mountain bunch of cattle at headquarters to combine them with the cattle already gathered and to get the bunch shaped up and ready for a trip to market. Yearlings had to be cut off from their mothers, a few old canner cows were to go also, and even some barren cows would be shipped. I felt sorry for the mother cows that stood around the pens after their calves had been cut off from them. Those cows would bawl and bawl for several days. They would not go out to graze, but would just mill around looking for their calves until finally hunger and despair would send them to the hills to forget their losses. "That is the way it must be; I must not let it hurt, I must steel myself like the men do, cast those feelings aside, mount my steed and ride away," I thought as I listened to the bawling echo through my mind. I knew that I would have to learn to tune out their cries. Again, I learned a lesson on my own, one that was forced upon me through the rugged life of a West Texas ranchwoman.

Once again the horses were shod, the chuck wagon prepared, and bedrolls stashed in sturdy tarps. We were ready to drive the herd to town. Our first night out was misery for me. The ground felt harder and harder as I lay in the bedroll on a flat place that Roy had cleared for our bed. I turned from side to side as my hipbones ached and a chill of the night air penetrated under the heavy suggins, or quilts. Roy told me to quit turning so I could get warm. I tried to settle my body, but I had to keep turning because my bones ached too badly for me to lie in one position for very long. What little sleep I got was very restless.

Just as daybreak came, Roy brought a large sotol plant close by and set it on fire. He had been up for some time drinking coffee with the other cowboys. The warmth of that sotol was like heaven and I dropped into a deep sleep, but I didn't enjoy that luxury for long. Roy soon came and handed me a cup of coffee, announcing, "We're ready to pull out."

As long as I live, I will never forget the wonderful feeling of warmth and comfort that burning sotol brought me as I lay in a cold and harsh bedroll.

The forty-six-mile cattle drive to Marathon, the nearest place for shipping cattle by railroad, was made in four days and three nights of camping. I thought it would be a great experience and fun, but I soon realized that that drive was a serious trip. Caution and care of the cattle were above all other things. The weights and conditions of the cattle were the deciding factors as to whether or not the year's proceeds from cattle sales would make expenses for another year of operation. Luckily, all hands were alert and expert at driving herds through rough country.

We did not suffer any stampedes; however, one was prevented by the quick action of Roy when he discovered a big black bear about to invade the herd. Roy had gone to look the herd over and see if all was quiet just at dusk when he saw the bear approaching the herd. Roy quickly chased him away and followed him as he lumbered up the mountain. Just as the bear climbed a bluff and was about to go over the top, Roy threw a loop that caught the bear around the neck. With a rope tied to the saddle horn on one end and to the bear on the other, Roy dragged him into our camp. I thought of a song that was popular to that time. Roy was riding a big black horse named Preacher, and the song "The Preacher and the Bear" was certainly appropriate to that event. This is the way I remember the song:

41

A Preacher and a Bear

Well, the preacher, he went out walking
It was on one Sunday morn.
'Course it was agin his religion
But he took his gun along.
Shot hisself some mighty fine quail
And one little measly hare,
And on the way returnin' home
He met a great big grizzly bear.

Well, the bear sat down
In the middle of the road
As mean as he could be.
And the preacher, he commenced to prayin'
As he climbed up a 'simmon tree.
And the bear looked up and he rolled his eyes
And he shook his ugly head.
And the preacher looked up to the skies
And these are the words he said.

Oh, Lord delivered Daniel from the lion's den.
Delivered Jonah from the belly of the whale.
And then
The Hebrew chillen from the fiery furnace
So the Good Book do declare!
Oh, Lord, Lord, if you can't help me
For goodness sake, don't you help that bear!
Oh, Lord, Lord, if you can't help me
For goodness sake, don't you help that bear!

I felt that those words were certainly true. The good Lord had not
helped that bear, and Roy had saved our herd from a stampede, which
could have extended our trip for many days.

One of the cowboys had a six-shooter handy and put a bullet in
the right spot, right between the bear's eyes. He dropped quickly to
the ground. The boys skinned the bear, but Roy did not feel that the
meat was edible and believed his carcass was of no use. He thought
that the only part worth keeping was the hide. Roy told me later that
he had killed many bears in his time and only out of necessity, but
he hated every one of those killings. He said that every time he skinned
one out and laid the carcass on the ground, it reminded him of a human being's skeleton.

Roy proposed that I take the bear hide to the taxidermist in Alpine
immediately because the hide would spoil. He said I should have a

rug made of it. I thought that was a great idea and early the next morning I was off to Alpine. When I reached Alpine, I headed straight for the taxidermist, left the hide, and returned as fast as I could back to Marathon. I stopped at our home in town to get a drink of water before going back to the herd. While I was in the house, I heard a knock on the door. When I opened the door I was face to face with the game warden, Dud Barker.

"Where's Roy?" he roared.

"He's with a herd of cattle about ten miles out," I stammered. I was petrified at the sight of Dud Barker, a gruff-looking man with a pistol buckled on his hip.

Again he bellowed, "Doesn't Roy know that it's against the law to kill a bear out of season?"

"Is it?" I asked. "I guess we didn't know."

"You tell Roy to come see me when he gets to town."

With that, he left me trembling and not knowing whether Roy would be hung on the spot or spend the balance of his life behind bars. I gathered my wits and quickly returned to the herd bearing the sad news of my encounter with Dud Barker. I could hardly get the story out to Roy. When Roy finally understood what I was trying to tell him, he became very angry and just stormed off toward the herd.

By noon the following day the cattle were penned in the stock pens at Marathon. From there they were loaded on the Southern Pacific Railroad cattle cars in which they were to be hauled to the cow market in San Antonio. What a relief it was to have finished up a month's hard work and know that the job was finally complete and well done! The next move was to get the chuck wagon and remuda back home, and Roy had to go see the game warden.

Dud Barker was friendly and kind enough to Roy; however, there was a twenty-five-dollar fine for killing a bear out of season. Ignorance of the law did not help one bit. Roy paid the fine and was soon ready to get back to the ranch where he was needed. Some of his ranch friends were incensed that Roy was fined for killing the bear under the circumstances; the herd could have been stampeded, and it would have taken weeks to gather them up in all that open country between town and the ranch.

Several of Roy's friends wanted him to fight the case. They tried to convince him that no jury in the world would find him guilty of a crime under those conditions. Friends offered to help fight the case and even offered him money, but Roy said that he would lose time and money, neither of which he could afford. Roy explained to his friends that he needed to get back to the ranch and forget about the fine. Roy was a man who made up his mind on his own and I never saw anyone who could change it.

I was mad at Dud Barker because he not only had frightened me but had fined Roy for what I felt was a right decision. Although I wanted to say my piece, I kept my mouth shut.

We closed the subject. Years later Roy and I became close friends with Dud Barker, who had resigned as game warden and had retired altogether. He was often seen sitting in the lobby of the Holland Hotel in Alpine, a place where many of us gathered to share tales and information. We soon found him to be a kind, good, and friendly person. We accepted the fact that he had only been doing his job as a lawman when he fined Roy, and we let the past remain the past. Roy held a few grudges, but he never held one against Dud.

Housecleaning

WE were all glad to be home again after the cow work. Even the little wood cookstove looked good to me after so many days in camp bending over a campfire for all our meals. One can appreciate a roof over one's head after spending days and nights in the open. I could not imagine how Roy could say that the happiest days of his life were when he lived under a hackberry tree. He even showed me the certain tree that he called home when he first came out of Mexico into the Big Bend of Texas and began working the open range. Since he had not establisted a homestead at that point, he kept a one-by-twelve piece of lumber wedged between limbs of the tree on which he kept a few groceries in a ten-gallon flour can, a bedroll, a coffee can, and a frying pan. He had even built a rock pen up against a high bluff to catch and hold horses. Yes, he was happy then, he was young, and he had no household responsibilities, and he had no one to answer to except himself. Riding, roping, and going where he pleased and when he pleased was a good life for Roy.

When he purchased land and a large cattle herd and had a one-room shack to call home and a wife to care for, Roy's life took on a large change. He knew that happiness would come in a different way and that there would probably be no more riding broncs just for the thrill of conquering the unknown.

"We need one more room," Roy remarked one day. "Winter is coming on, so I think we'll build a comfortable room onto the one we have.

I will get Gus Voss, the windmill man, to build a large bedroom onto this kitchen."

"I can hardly wait," I told him. "I'm getting mighty tired of sleeping in that bedroll on the kitchen floor."

Roy made good his promise, and before long I had a bedroom, a good bed, and a nice dresser. I fashioned some curtains for the window out of flour sacks and I then indeed felt that I was living in the lap of luxury.

One morning I heard Roy tell Lee and Jona that they would be working on the corrals across the Maravillas. I asked Roy if I might stay at the house as I would not be needed. I promised that if any trouble came up, I would yell, as they would be in hearing distance. Roy agreed and I was left alone for the day.

What I had in mind was to clean up the place, which I did in a big way. I swept, scrubbed, dusted, and worked on anything and everything, including the old black coffee pot. That particular coffee pot had never been cleaned before. The men always threw out the coffee grounds, rinsed the pot with cold water, and considered it ready to set down on the fire at any given moment to brew a fresh pot of coffee.

I decided to take this pot to the sand pile, scrub it with sand first, scrub it with wood ashes, and then scrub it some more. I did not have any other kind of cleaning material except soap. I finally removed the crusts of black from the outside and most of the stains on the inside. I was more than proud of my accomplishment.

In the kitchen, there was writing all over the walls and door facings. Those scriptures were something like this: "Rained big on July 10th," "Bought 6 bulls from Hess," "Set hen on Mar. 5th," "Trip to river May 3," and other such writings. I thought the room would look much better with these writings all gone. I only left the sign on the kitchen door: "Help yourself to grub, wash dishes, put cat out."

When Roy and the men came home that night, they did not praise my clean kitchen. The first words I heard were, "Hell – she's washed away our records, how are we to remember everything?" Roy complained, "We depend on these records to settle arguments!"

I sat silently while Roy and the other men glared at those clean walls with frustration. It was as though a fire had swept away some valuable information for good. However, to this day I fail to see why those notes were so important. I had only wanted to be a good housekeeper.

The next morning when I awakened I heard grumbling sounds coming from the kitchen. Four men were sitting in a torment as they sipped on the early morning coffee. It was obvious that they were trying to make the best of a bad situation. I heard Lee moan, "It will be six months before this pot can make decent coffee again."

I knew then that I had made another bad mistake. I would never be forgiven for washing that coffee pot. I covered my head with a pillow and sank down under the covers as Roy came into the bedroom. "Here, try to drink this coffee. Why in the hell did you wash the coffee pot?"

I had always enjoyed lying in a comfortable bed and listening to the cowboys as they ground the Arbuckle coffee beans in the coffee grinder as they prepared the morning meal. That particular morning I was not so comfortable. The grumbling about the clean coffee pot did not last the six months as predicted, and the men were thoughtful enough to keep their comments to themselves so that I would not feel so bad. I never even attempted to wash that coffee pot again or scrub those walls without first checking with Roy.

Even though I was somewhat embarrassed about my mistake, I felt that it was just a little one. Needless to say, the story was told in Alpine and Marathon, and it was years before I heard the end of it. Roy's friends would casually ask if I had washed the coffee pot again and then let out a hearty laugh. Let a woman make one little mistake and it becomes the joke of years.

I was proud of my newly cleaned home and much more comfortable with the addition. I had spent many hours presenting a home that was comfortable and pleasant for Roy and me as well as those who lived with us or visited us. I still felt that one more addition was necessary, but I was a little afraid of asking Roy about it. I wanted a beautiful porch on which all could sit and look at the gorgeous mountains, the sunset, and Maravillas Canyon and hear the birds sing in the distance. I knew this was too much to ask, so instead I approached Roy with the suggestion of adding an arbor to the front of the house. I explained to Roy that it would be a much cooler place to sit and we would all enjoy its comfort.

Roy accepted the suggestion rather quickly and soon Roy and the men were building my dream arbor. They first built the structure and supports and then covered the top of the arbor with sotol poles. Upon those poles they placed candelilla, a plant native to this area. This weed provided a shade from the burning sun and kept the area under the arbor shaded most of the day. It was the perfect arbor in no time.

I planted vines on the sides of the arbor that grew and provided additional shade, and I kept the dirt floor under it swept and moist

9. Hallie's favorite place in the early years on the ranch; this arbor was the coolest spot around during the hot summers

so that it was always ready for visitors or family. Roy took a ten-gallon tin can and surrounded it with tow sacks that were attached with baling wire. After completely covering the can with those sacks, he filled the open areas through the sacks and around the can with oats. He clamped a wire to this can and hung it from the arbor top. Roy pulled a gourd from a patch near the house and cleaned it out. After letting it dry in the sun for some time, he tied a piece of twine around its neck and hooked it to a piece of wire that wrapped around the can. This gourd became the dipper from which many of us drank cool refreshing water. Each evening Roy would fill this can with water and wet the sacks and oats down. This process kept the water cool for drinking at all times. Many a cowboy's thirst was quenched from this can.

We also kept a basin where all the workers or visitors could wash up before a meal. This kept the mess of the soap and water outside. All in all, the arbor was my favorite part of the ranch house, and I and many others spent numerous hours under its shade and enjoyed its beauty. I often got compliments on its charm and it soon became the favorite spot of all who visited.

Most of my free time was spent enjoying the peace and tranquility that the arbor provided, but I did enjoy a few other hobbies, such as gathering the arrowheads or other Indian artifacts that were prevalent on the ranch. I came by this pleasure quite innocently and I think that Roy often felt that it was just another means of my wasting good working time, although I really think that he did not mind my "foolish" jaunts or huntings. I did learn to avoid doing these things when Roy was working hard or apt to be displeased with my interests. I spent much more time working with the men than I did enjoying my idle time and that made Roy much happier with me.

As we added to the house and I picked up new hobbies, I found that living on the ranch was wonderful. It was through those new hobbies that I got relief from the everyday stress of ranch life, a life that was exciting, happy, and adventurous, as well as stressful.

Indian Campground

Roy and the boys were trailing for home late one evening after a long day's work, and I was lagging behind and feeling weary to the bone. The sun was almost down, just right to make long shadows and magnify every rock and every track. I happened to notice a black shining piece of rock that looked quite different, so I got off my horse and picked it up. I knew immediately that it was something that had been in the hands of others by the way it had been shaped and worked upon. At supper that night I showed the rock to Roy and the boys and asked them what they thought about it.

Roy said, "That's an Indian spearhead." He then explained that our entire ranch was an Indian campground with Indian shelters, large mounds, and even a painting on a bluff not too far from the house.

Immediately I was interested in the things Roy was telling me. I thought to myself, "I'll explore this ranch and learn something about these unknown people who dwelled here some time in the past."

Shortly after this incident, I began to explore the many rock shelters that had smoked ceilings and cracked rocks out in front. I found many crude arrowheads, scraping knives, and tools of all kinds. At least five figures, resembling bears of some sort, were plainly drawn with some kind of red coloring on the walls of a cave. The coloring was not paint but probably cinnabar, which is a red rock often found in West Texas. Near these paintings was a rock shelter with many large boulders that had crude markings on them. It appeared that these markings were worn slick from human hands touching them or human bodies sitting on them. There I found many Indian artifacts and Indian potholes where grain or something like it had been ground. All the evidence showed that probably ten thousand or more years ago a tribe or many tribes through the centuries had dwelled there. As I extended my explorations in the Maravillas Shut-up, I was amazed at the many caves that showed evidence of occupation. I was charmed by all of this rare and interesting history of our ranch. Roy said that every time I was really needed to hunt cows, I was off my horse looking for arrowheads and rocks.

I began to make a study of these unknown people who were of an earlier age and so mystical to me. Roy, who had known many Indians in northern Mexico as well as along the Rio Grande border, said that they knew nothing of these early people; that all these signs were there when they came. The more I explored the ranch looking for an explanation for the smoked caves with tons and tons of chipped rocks, ashes, and charcoal in front of them, the more interested I became in the wonders on the ranch. I knew that I should have been looking for cows, but more and more I wanted to explore. I found many large *metates*, too heavy for me to carry, so I asked Jona to bring them into the house for me. But there was a large boulder in one of the shelters that would stay right where it was as long as I had any say-so. This rare artifact was as large as a dining room table and had many markings on it. In the center of this huge boulder was a *molcajete*, a rounded-out hole some ten inches in diameter and about eighteen inches deep. The grinding stone was still in it. As I examined this "workbench," as I called it, I thought to myself, "I am the first and only white woman to see these wonderful artifacts. Here I stand in the shade of this cave where some thousands and thousands of years ago people of some kind dwelled for years and years, and now here I am."

After I had spent many hours exploring in the Indian shelters and neglecting my cowboy duties, I heard Jona and Lee discussing my activities.

Lee was commenting, "Hallie has gone plum loco over this Indian stuff – do you think she's getting tired of helping with the cows?"

Jona, in his casual way, said, "I seen her climbing those canyon walls, going into dark caves, scratching around in those mounds of soot and cracked rock like she was hunting for gold or something. I wonder why Roy lets her go off like that in those bluffs. She'll get hurt one of these days."

"Did you notice how dreamy-eyed and quiet she is when she comes in from the canyon? She looks like she's seen a ghost or been talking to the rocks. I don't understand women!" said Jona. "They sure can do fool things."

Lee nodded in agreement.

Roy was patient with me about the Indian caves and agreed that I could go to Alpine and talk with V. J. Smith, a professor at Sul Ross University, and find out from him about these early people. V. J. Smith had made a study of the early people of the Big Bend and helped me find some material about them; however, there was not much that anyone knew. The more I read and studied, the less I knew about the people, when they were there, how long they stayed, and where they went. I searched for burial grounds, I dug in mounds, but found nothing much. I could only draw my own conclusions. My imagination kept me highly entertained.

In my travels, Roy showed me a particular place where rocks and stones were obviously placed in some type of pattern. I often went there and attempted to figure out some rhyme or reason for the stones being placed in this manner. Around this patterning, there were paths leading into the center of the pattern, paths that had been used for so long that no vegetation grew in their trenches. Two paths came together and formed an apex; I thought that at one time this must have pointed to something in the mountains, but Roy and I ruled that idea out and decided that the point was not a marker. Some of the rock clusters formed circles and some formed rectangles; others formed squares. Each cluster was a pile of rocks placed very carefully in position.

I remained confused, and the more confused I became, the more interested I became in finding answers. I took my first questions to V. J. Smith and soon various other archeologists and geologists were coming to the ranch to investigate this strange pattern left by some earlier people. Unfortunately, no one came up with or has come up with an answer to this pattern, which somewhat resembles Stonehenge. Roy and I decided that it must have been some type of ceremonial grounds, and of course we named it just that, a name that remains in use today. This place still draws people who are interested in earlier cavemen (some archeologists claim that this civilization was tens of thousands of years old) and Indians (other archeologists claim these people were Indians), but all who see it know that it is a place with some special meaning.

The ranch needed much work to keep it in full operation, but it offered me many types of entertainment. I never missed town much, as I was always finding new and interesting objects, plants, artifacts, caves, and so on that would grab my interest, and I would soon be off in my own little world again.

World War I

WORLD War I had taken its toll on many West Texas families. For four years, I had watched many friends and locals leave to help fight for our country. Because so many men were needed to fight, there was a shortage of men to work the area's ranches. By 1918, the West Texas ranches were suffering, but fortunately Roy had not been called due to his age of forty years. I was thankful for that, as I was not prepared to run the ranch alone.

Our boys were leaving for the service as fast as they could be inducted. My brother Frank, who was the eldest of us six Crawford children, was called to serve in August, 1918. He was inducted into the navy and stationed in South Carolina in November of that same year for training when he contracted the Spanish influenza, now called the flu. He was ill for only a few days when he developed pneumonia. He battled the trying virus but his strength, somewhat weakened by his long days and nights in the service, could not prevail.

Mama had been really worried because she had not heard from Frank for such a long time. After several long weeks she received a letter from him explaining that he had been ill with something that many of the servicemen were contracting. He said in his letter that he was somewhat better and expected to serve on guard duty that very night. Although Mama was glad to hear from him, she was still worried. Roy and I were with her when she got Frank's letter and we felt much better. We decided to leave Mama and go on to the ranch, yet I could tell that she was in no way satisfied with the report.

The trip to the ranch took us all day from Alpine and we were extremely tired when we got home, so we went directly to bed. I awoke the next morning to a neighbor knocking on the door bearing extremely sad news.

The day Frank's letter had arrived in Alpine, another correspondence was also delivered to Mama. This telegram bore the return address of the president of the United States. Mama shakily opened the telegram and read that the United States president was sorry to inform our family that Frank was dead. In the telegram was also the plan for the return of Frank's body. Mama immediately sent word to Roy and me at the ranch.

Roy and I loaded everything into the car and headed back to Alpine. When we got there, our family was in a state of shock. Frank's death was our first real family loss, and all of us were greatly affected. Somehow we managed to get through the rough time.

51

The day of Frank's burial was a somber and very sad one for our entire family. The hardest part for me was seeing my parents grieve so much. They had always appeared so strong, and this tragedy really took some spirit from my mother. This was actually the second encounter with death that had involved Frank and his family, and Mama felt that she had lost so much.

Frank had married Nona Garnett in Alpine just before he was inducted into the service. The couple had a baby girl, Lorena, soon after their marriage and were very happy. When Lorena was six months old, Nona had an attack of appendicitis. The local country doctor was immediately called. When he got there, he knew that her case was serious. He promptly placed her upon the dining room table (a custom of the time for surgery) and began to operate. He had barely begun the operation when Nona gave up her life. When Frank was inducted into the service, he left his baby daughter Lorena with her maternal grandparents, Walter and Mamie Garnett. He planned to return for her, but after he died as well she was reared by grandparents and never knew either of her parents. Our family always stayed in close contact with Lorena, and we knew that she was well cared for and given love, attention, and a good education by her grandparents.

Of course, our service boys were in cramped quarters in quickly erected camps all over the country. The facilities were crowded, the food scarce, the equipment poor, and the medical facilities limited. Frank was one of the first victims of the flu and it was strange that it was a germ rather than a bullet that killed him. In fact, many of our men were stricken with this new influenza, and many died from it. It, along with the war, certainly took a toll on our American men. It was a time I'll never forget.

A few weeks after Frank's death, our own Tuff Hatch was called to serve. Roy had depended on Tuff as a cowhand since he was twelve years old and was really worried about Tuff's leaving. Tuff had a few head of cattle that Roy had given him in place of pay. Tuff had raised this herd from calves and held a great pride in his little collection. We all knew that Tuff had great dreams of becoming a successful cattleman himself. He really hated to leave his "family."

Since Tuff was leaving and the unknown was ahead, Roy bought back the cattle from Tuff, placed him on the train in Marathon with several other local boys who had been called, and bade him goodbye. This goodbye was very difficult for Roy, who looked at Tuff as a son.

Tuff returned to Marathon after the war was over but did not return to the ranch. Roy and I never knew why Tuff did not return, but we suspected that he was already too ill to work. Shortly after his return, Tuff died from the ills that scarred him during the war.

Tuff's leaving had left us shorthanded, and in the meantime, Bob Breeding, a very mature man and one of Roy's friends, came to the ranch to live with us and help with the chores around the ranch. Bob was an educated man and highly respected by all who knew him. He had been a successful ranchman, but after an unhappy marriage he had sold his ranch and become a worldwide traveler who invested in different ventures, sometimes making a great deal of money, sometimes losing everything he owned. It was after a big loss that he came to be with us. He just wanted a home. Uncle Bob, as we called him, soon became my good friend and helped me over many hard times. I always felt that I had close friends at the ranch and around the area, but it was some time before I really developed any friendships in town.

Roy and I had always used the house in town for a stopping place, but we were married for quite a while before I began to call it home. I liked the house and spent quite a bit of my time fixing curtains and arranging the rooms to my liking. I was always busy when we were in town and did not think for a minute that I was being ignored by the neighbors on our street. Roy and I had our good ranch neighbors, the Buttrills, who lived on their ranch some sixteen miles south of Marathon. Lou and Margaret Buttrill had been Roy's lifelong friends, and as a schoolgirl in Alpine I had had a close relationship with their two daughters, Marion and Lou Anna. I treasured the friendship of the Buttrill family.

We also enjoyed the friendships of the Louie Ritchey and Feron Ritchey families. They had been my friends in Alpine for several years before they moved to Marathon and put in a general merchandise store. With my move to Marathon, our friendships were reinstated.

Vernon and Vivian McIntire, also ranchers, were also my friends and were always nice to Roy and me. They never forgot to include us in their social activities, which were fairly frequent. In fact, Vivian McIntire invited me to my first party in Marathon, which helped me feel welcome and accepted.

Even though the war was raging through the world, we tried to maintain some stability at home. We kept close friends and depended on one another during rough times. Friends became very important to me even though my life revolved mostly around Roy and the ranch.

After several trips to Marathon and being in our home in town, I noticed that the neighbors on our street were avoiding me as though I had the plague. Those neighbors who lived on both sides of us would

10. Hallie at house in town, 1930

pass by and stare at the house, but if I appeared at the door or was in the yard, they quickly looked the other way. One day I said to Roy, "What do you suppose is wrong with all the neighbors on this street? They don't speak to me or come to see me."

Roy explained that they did not need anyone else in their lives. They were all kin to one another and all wrapped up in one another. Roy also said, "Besides that, you're a schoolteacher from Alpine."

He told me that for many years there had been some jealousies between the two towns. He said that at one time Marathon people were happy to be in Buschel County, which is now Brewster County. I didn't exactly understand what Roy's remark meant, and I asked him to explain.

"Well, it started a long time ago." he responded. He told me how the problems between the two towns began. Many years ago, all of this West Texas area was one large county, Presidio County, and its county seat was Fort Davis. This system worked amicably for years, or at least until the railroad came through this part of the country.

As the story goes, according to "town talk," many people were upset because the railroad did not have a depot in Fort Davis, yet the county seat remained there. A few men in Marfa really pushed to move the county seat to their town. Of course, the people in Fort Davis did not agree. At some point, these few men confiscated the Fort Davis records and hid them at some ranch where no one could get to them.

While the records were missing, Marfa was erecting a courthouse of its own. Soon after it was completed, the missing records appeared in the new courthouse and Marfa, very underhandedly as some say, became the county seat.

This little scam did not set well with the people in Alpine or Marathon. Both of these towns also wanted to be known as the county seat. Someone came up with the idea that Marathon, Alpine, and the lower Big Bend should be divided into three counties with Marathon, the centrally located town, being the county seat for Buschel County. The three counties were to be Buschel, Foley, and Brewster. For some time it appeared that this system would be accepted – that is, until a man named Wigfall Van Sickle got involved.

Van Sickle was a prominent attorney in Alpine and had quite a bit of influence on many people. He did not approve of the new division and very quickly made a trip to Austin where he met with the Texas legislature. Shortly after his trip, the people of our area found out that Brewster County had been developed with Alpine as its county seat, and the counties of Buschel and Foley had been abolished.

As Roy finished telling the above story in his fashion, he slowly turned to me and said, "Now do you understand the rivalry between the two towns?"

I just nodded my head, as I did not need any more explanation.

"Now Hon," Roy cautioned. "Just bide your time and pay no attention to them. You have other friends, and we'll get along just fine."

I heeded Roy's advice and went along with my own business, forgetting about the next-door neighbors. This experience was new to me; in Alpine I had always been a part of the "gang" with never a thought of being ignored. I did have some problem accepting or forgetting my neighbors' attitudes toward me even though Roy thought it best to ignore them.

After several weeks of being in and out of town, I decided that I needed something to pass my time while I was in town. When Roy and I came to town, I usually stayed at the house while he tended to business. I chose to piece a quilt in my spare time and then finish it by stitching it nicely with quilting stitches. Now, I had never put a quilt in quilting frames, but had seen my mother put in many, so I had some idea of how to proceed. That I did, and in no time I had frames built, hung from the wall, and my new quilt ready for stitching. This process took up a lot of room, so I used our back proch for the project.

One afternoon as I was quilting away, I heard a knock at the front door. I walked to the door and was surprised to see the caller being no other than Millie Simpson from two houses down the street. The dowager Millie Simpson was the Marathon matriarch of the street. I knew that all those who lived on that street were kin and that "Aunt Millie" was the boss. I was wondering what on earth she was doing at my front door.

"I am Millie Simpson from down the street," she said.

"Come in and have a chair," I murmured, not knowing whether she was friend or foe.

As she walked across the living room, she was eyeing everything in the house, and she chose a spot to sit where she could see most of the house, which she scrutinized carefully as we sat. I finally composed myself enough to mention that I was busy on the back porch quilting.

"Oh!" exclaimed Millie, "I'll help you. Let me see your quilt."

We went to the porch and I showed her the small amount of quilting that I had done. "My work is very crude and stitches too long, but I'm trying." As she looked at my work, I became ashamed of showing it to her. But then she sat down, picked up a needle, and started stitching on the quilt. Her stitches were beautiful and very even. She was quilting very fast and appeared to be enjoying what she was doing. At first I just watched.

As we began talking she said, "I'm going to show you how to make smaller stitches. It'll be much better, and I'm going to help you finish this quilt." As she talked and worked, I sized her up and decided that she was going to be a good neighbor and friend. We worked the balance of the evening and chatted away on various subjects, and we both enjoyed the visit and stitching.

The following day "Aunt" Millie and her daughter-in-law, Edie Granger, who lived next door to me, came to my house, Then came Fannie Harris, another of the neighbors. They all showed up with needles and thimbles in hand, and we all soon had my quilt finished and ready to take out of the frame. Millie offered to bind the quilt for me, which I was glad to have her do. After the completion of the quilt, I thought to myself, "I am IN!" That was a great feeling.

I no longer felt that I was "that schoolteacher from Alpine." I knew that I was a part of the neighborhood, a friend, and finally, Roy's wife. I thought how funny that such friendships started over a small quilt.

Thief in the Neighborhood

Roy was anxious to get back to the ranch, so I had little time to spend with my new acquaintances. As we were readying ourselves to return to the ranch, I noticed that the peach tree in our front yard was loaded with peaches. I talked Roy into helping me pick several bushels to take home with us. He did so reluctantly and at the last minute before we loaded up for the ranch. On our way home I made plans for those peaches.

Once at the ranch and after we had unloaded, I decided to make peach preserves. I asked Lee, Jona, and Roy to help me peel the fruit. That was my first experience in preserving anything. I was more than proud of those preserves and put the filled jars on a shelf for display. Every day, we would look at those pretty preserves thinking that they were too precious to eat.

One day Jona went to the river to look for some of our stray cows and Lee stayed at the house while Roy and I took a trip to town. We stayed longer in town than expected, so Lee came to town to see what had delayed us. As Lee arrived in town, Roy and I were ready to head back to the ranch. Lee decided that since he had made the trip to town, he would stay for a few days. Roy and I left Lee and returned to the ranch.

The first thing I noticed when Roy and I walked into the kitchen was a jar of preserves missing. I said to Roy, "Lee ate preserves while we were in town."

Roy replied, "I guess he was hungry and I suppose we need to eat them sometime."

"Sure," I replied. "It's all right with me. I just hate to see our display broken up."

When Lee returned to the ranch, he noticed that a jar of preserves were gone and he told us some time later that he thought to himself, "Roy and Hallie ate preserves while I was in town."

When Jona came back from his river trip, I decided to open a jar of preserves in celebration of our being all together and at home once again. As Jona heaped his plate with preserves, he remarked, "I ate some preserves just like these in Coble's camp yesterday."

I looked at Lee and Lee looked at me. "So *that's* where the preserves went," I said. "I thought Lee had eaten the preserves, and I guess Lee thought that Roy and I had eaten them." We all had a big laugh.

While we were discussing Coble and his "taking" ways, we all remembered the time when our good neighbors, Charlie and Tom Green, were running their fall chuck wagon for a cow work. All the neighbors were on the work in case some of their cattle were mixed in the herd. Of course Coble came even though he had no cattle in the area; the free food from the chuck wagon was always a temptation to him. Everyone was busy with the herd, branding, marking, and cutting out their cows. All hands were busy except Coble.

Charlie Green needed more vaccine so he dashed back to the chuck box to get the needed bottle. As he approached the chuck box, he saw Coble sneaking away with some knives and forks. Coble did not see Charlie and certainly did not expect anyone to be around.

When Charlie saw what Coble was doing, it made him so angry that he couldn't see straight. He couldn't find anything to hit him with, so he picked up a handful of rocks and started chunking them at Coble. As Coble ran with knives and forks in hand, Charlie continued to throw rocks at him until he could no longer reach him with his aim. When Coble was out of throwing distance, he stopped running and shouted to Charlie, "come see us sometime, Charlie."

"Yep," said Lee now, "Coble will take anything he can. I remember when he took some clothes that had been hung in the sun to dry off Mrs. Henderson's clothes line. And, he also robbed all the hens' nests at the Henderson Ranch!"

Jona chimed in, "The customs officers caught Coble crossing a horse out of Mexico and made him return it. A feller like Coble ought to be run out of the country."

I thought to myself, "Yes, Coble was up to his usual tricks of helping himself to other ranchers' supplies." We all knew that he would sit over on a hill watching us as we would ride off for the day, and he would then sneak into our house and take a little dab of beans, a cup of lard, and a small amount of flour and coffee. He would then go by the barn and pick up a few horseshoes and nails. That was just the way he lived; taking a little at a time from all the neighboring ranches. Every now and then he would steal a cow or calf. Roy was beginning to get tired of Coble's "taking ways," and after he stole our milch calf, Roy decided to do something about the man's habits. He met him on the road one day and finally had a talk with him.

"I ought to kill you, but you're not worth killing," said Roy.

"Why Roy, what are you talking about?" he responded.

"You're a damn thief – that's what I'm talking about!"

"Roy, you know I wouldn't steal, by godda!"

"You've been stealing ever since you came to this country. You stole my milch calf, you've stolen groceries, you killed and butchered one of my cows at Dove Mountain, and all of these things are enough to send you to the pen."

"I did not butcher your cow," he stammered.

"Oh, yes you did!" shouted Roy. "Jim Manning was with you when you did it, and he told me all about it."

"Well, I wouldn't a thought Jim woulda told it, by godda."

At that time Roy became good and mad and continued to inform Coble of all the thieving acts he had committed in the surrounding neighborhood. He reminded him that he was not worth killing, and that if he was sent to the pen, his family would starve to death. Roy offered the man an alternative.

"Coble, I want you to leave this country. If I ever see you here or near this place again, I will personally kill you."

Coble knew that Roy meant what he said. Coble left, and we didn't see him again in our part of the country.

We often spent our mealtimes discussing events of the days or tales of interest. Of course, the tales of Coble were always amusing and almost everyone enjoyed them. Even though he was a thief, he did little personal harm to anyone and gave many of us entertaining stories to listen to and tell.

First Holidays

INTO the early month of December of our first year of marriage Roy remarked, "You should see the Chisos Mountains now that the cold has turned the leaves into their winter colors. If you think the spring flowers are pretty, you should see the fall colors."

"Let's go!" I replied, and prepared to venture toward the mountains. We jumped in our Super-6 and headed for the hills. As we chugged along over the rough and rocky road headed toward the

Chisos Mountains, Roy pointed out places that were a part of his earlier days.

"Over there to your right is Bone Springs, where my father once lived after leaving his ranch in Mexico. He kept a watering place at the springs for the mules and burros that hauled ore from the mines in Mexico. He charged five cents per animal for water. Then, looking over here to your left is Dog Canyon. Do you see that crack in the mountain a little farther down? That's Devil's Den. There are places in that canyon that are so narrow and deep the sun never shines."

I was amazed at all those places as Roy pointed them out to me. I realized again how beautiful the country really was.

As we drove along, Roy continued, "We're near McKinney Springs. Now you can see Tornillo Flat and the Tornillo Creek. I used to cut tobosa grass in the flat for my saddle horses. See ahead of us? That's Roy's Peak. I was ranching there when Arthur Stiles and Stuart Penick were putting names on the map of this country." Roy explained that these two men had their camp there with him when Roy had just left Mexico and before he set up the Dove Mountain place, and that they had become good friends. Roy went on, "Early one morning as the sun came up over Dead Horses Mountain, Arthur was busy working on a map. He looked up as the first ray of sunshine reached the peak and said, 'We'll call this peak Roy's Peak.'"

As we drove along, Roy and I decided to go on to Boquillas and visit with Chata and Juan Sada, who were longtime friends of Roy's. Chata and Roy had been childhood playmates while the Stillwells ranched in Mexico. Juan Sada owned and operated a silver mine near Boquillas. Chata was noted for her good Mexican food and her charming personality. Roy and I had a marvelous visit with Chata and Juan and enjoyed a delicious meal. Afterwards, we returned to the ranch.

Just around the corner was Thanksgiving, which had always meant much to me. Turkey, dressing, cranberry sauce, cakes, and pies always came to mind as I thought of this holiday. As the day drew nearer I insisted that we go to Marathon to celebrate. I wanted to cook a turkey. Roy agreed, and off to town we went. Roy purchased the largest turkey he could find – and the problem of cooking it began. Neither of us knew the first principle of cooking a turkey. After we killed the turkey, scalded it, and picked the feathers off of it, we discovered that it was too large to fit into our oven. Roy said that we were not to worry – he would find a way to cook it. He filled a big tin can with water, built a big fire in the yard, put the turkey in the can, placed the can over the fire and boiled the turkey for hours. It did not taste like the turkey that Mama cooked, though, but I certainly didn't tell Roy this. Roy said as we ate that turkey, "I'm not too crazy about turkey, I'd really rather have a goat to eat." Anyway, we enjoyed the festivities surrounding that holiday even if the meal was not the best.

Roy and I stayed in Marathon until Christmas of that year. We busied ourselves in the preparations for the upcoming holidays. Those preparations were as important to me as the holidays themselves.

Mama and Papa insisted that we spend the Christmas holidays with them in Alpine. Roy and I had many friends in Alpine, and we knew that there would be some goat ropings and dances for us to attend. Those events were always a fun time for us. So we headed to Alpine a few days before Christmas. We intended to stay through Christmas and return to Marathon for New Year's Day and a big dance.

Just as we were preparing to head back to Marathon, a huge snow fell. There was no way we could return to Marathon. We made one attempt to get through the deep snow but only got about two miles before we had to turn around. Roy, having already spent more time in town than he preferred, became anxious. I knew what to expect – room 205 at the Holland Hotel was going to receive guests. "My, my, if those walls could talk. What a story!" I thought as Roy began to get ready to leave. This particular room was never rented to travelers or to hotel guests. It was reserved for those locals who wished to play in a game of chance, luck, science – in other words, poker. In order to participate in one of those games, one must have at least one hundred dollars in gold or silver. Paper money was usually not accepted.

I never did stand in Roy's way when he got the urge to join the boys in a game of poker. I realized that Roy was a hardworking ranchman and suffered many trying times. He needed to "blow off steam" once in a while with the boys in a friendly game. Winning or losing was not so important; the game was mainly an outlet for him. I had my relaxation playing bridge, hunting arrowheads, or quilting. Roy had his poker games with his longtime ranch friends.

There were times when I sat in the lobby of the hotel waiting for Roy to come down the stairs from room 205 so we could go home. I never became impatient, and many times on our trips home from those games Roy would tell me who had lost, who had won, and who had bet what. Sometimes Roy came out a winner, sometimes a loser; however, win or lose Roy always seemed to enjoy those games.

I mentioned to him one time, "The same money makes its rounds among you players and at least it stays among friends. Maybe one has the winnings for a time, then someone else will have them. It's all in the game with the money just moving around and around, isn't it?"

Roy just laughed and said, "That's how you women look at it!"

As the snow continued to fall, Roy left with his pocket full of money. He was gone for a day and a night. When he returned to Mama's house, his pockets were full to the brim. He had even won several dollar bills, something that had no value whatsoever to Roy. After making several remarks about that poker game, he stated that he was disappointed that there were men there using that "worthless paper money." He told of his winnings, and he gave the "worthless" dollar bills to my younger sister, Glen. How she loved to have Roy come around because she knew those dollar bills could be spent even though he thought they would buy nothing.

The next day, the snow had melted enough, we had had enough holiday spirit and visiting, and were homesick enough that we took off for our home in Marathon, which was the next best thing to home at the ranch.

We had not been in Marathon long when I realized that I was going to have a baby. I quickly told Roy about the expected arrival and he said that he was "tickled to death!" He told me he wanted many children, especially a son. I was just hoping for a healthy baby.

Having been accepted in the town neighborhood and on my way to being a mother, I experienced a strange feeling. I thought that I could never again be just a careless young girl and think only of myself. I was to be responsible for another life. There was no turning back at that point. I saw life from a different angle and it was nothing like the ideas that I had while growing up. I remembered telling my sister that I would not have children, raise chickens, cook or wash dishes, or even keep a house. I wanted to joyride, dance, and go places for fun. I had said I would cut my cakes, pies, and bread while hot and let everyone eat them while fresh and steaming. My mother never let us children do this because they would all be gone too quickly. Also, I said that I would take my nap in the afternoons on the bed. Mama always made us children make a pallet on the floor for our daytime naps. We were not allowed on the bed in the daytime unless we were sick. I was sure I would not sew; I would buy all my dresses ready-made. Mama had always made my clothes, and while they were pretty and nice I longed for ready-mades. I also told myself that when I got married and on my own, I would dance until midnight. My sister and I had lived by a curfew, and Mama had a striking clock. I soon realized that my dreams were not to be and that changes in my life were already being made. I learned quickly that life was not a dream and all those promises I had made to myself soon had to be "eaten."

While I was getting my town house in order and mulling over the fact that I was going to have a baby, Roy was celebrating with the men in town. Domino games at the local "Bloody Bucket," the only beer joint, took place during the day, and quite often at night a poker game at some friend's house would entertain the men. In the meantime, Syl Adams, one of Roy's best friends, sold a bunch of calves and bought himself a new Buick. Syl was more than proud of his Buick and boasted to Roy that his Buick could outrun Roy's Hudson Super-6. Now, Roy was just as proud of his car as Syl was of his. Naturally, a bet was made.

It just so happened that at that same time the town's favorite bootlegger had hit town with a load of sotol, tequila, and *aguardiente*. Word spread that a big car race was soon to be run between Roy with his Hudson Super-6 and Syl with his Buick. The race was to start in the west end of Marathon at "Fussy Flats" and would run parallel with the railroad tracks, past the stock pens, and on through town to the old Guayule Plant.

Early in the morning on the day set for the race, a crowd started gathering and looking over the fine cars. They were trying to decide on which car to place their bets. Noon came, betting was still underway, and drinks were plentiful. Most men wanted to share their bottles, there was good fellowship all around, great jokes were told, and expensive bets were made in real old-time cowboy fashion. Finally, time slipped by and the sun was starting on the downgrade, shadows were getting longer, and it was decided that the race should get underway.

While the men were readying themselves for the race, and unknown to them, a medicine show had come to town and the peddler had put up a tent in the pathway of the race. He had set up medicine bottles, pots and pans, and all the things that would often sell to country people. The medicine man was proud of his wares and took great pains in fixing the attractive displays. Plenty of Cura-Cura salve, Arnica salve, Calomel, Dr. La Gear's Horse liniment, Lydia Pinkham elixir (good for "ladies' ailments"), Baby Percy talcum powder, paregoric, and asafetida were among his many wares. (Most of us knew that the only reason the asafetida worked was because the smell was so bad that no one would dare come around you if you were wearing it; therefore, you were never exposed to contagious illnesses.) When the medicine man came to town, he was a very popular caller, and many peo-

63

ple purchased goods of all sorts from him. Many times the medicine man held contests to promote sales, the most frequent being a contest to identify the most popular woman in town. People would pay a penny for a certain number of votes. I remember that Paz Valenzuela won one of those contests and received a diamond ring. Not only did the townspeople need the wares that the medicine man sold, but they enjoyed his visits immensely, as they were great entertainment. It didn't take long for the medicine man to get his business going that day. People crowded around as soon as he set up shop.

Meanwhile, on the upper end of the racetrack a loud boom from Louie Ritchey's six-shooter was the signal that the race had started, and the crowd of onlookers who had made handsome bets ran as fast as they could to watch the racing cars. Syl and Roy, in a dead heat, did not see the medicine show tent that loomed in their pathway. When they discovered the obstacle, it was too late to avoid a smashup. As the two drivers emerged from under the overturned tent, they blinked their bloodshot eyes as they encountered a furious old man who was waving his arms and shouting, "I'll sue you blankety blanks! Where's the sheriff here?"

Roy rose to his full six feet two inches and declared that he was the sheriff.

"I'll sue!" yelled the old man. "Where is the county judge?"

At that moment Syl said, "I'm the judge here."

At that, Syl offered the old man a drink from his sotol bottle. By that time the crowd of onlookers had arrived at the scene and they too offered drinks to the angry old man.

"It's a plumb shame," commented Bill Fudge as he viewed the medicine bottles, pots and pans, and trinkets that were scattered around in piles on the ground. "Have a drink of this tequila and we'll pick up this stuff and put the tent together again."

While the men were putting the tent back up and arranging the displays of medicine bottles and other items, the angry old medicine man was being treated to free drinks from various sotol bottles.

"The tent is fixed and everything's back into place," announced Speck Harris as he viewed the contents in the tent.

The old man rose to his feet, blinked his watery eyes at the battered tent, and in a loud voice shouted, "Give me another drink, boys, back up, and run through her again."

The race was never finished and the bets were never paid. To this day, no one really knows which car was the fastest.

Roy and Syl were always competitive but remained the best of friends. On one particular trip to Alpine from Marathon, Roy was leading the way. Roy enjoyed always proving that his car was the best. As he scurried along, he would glance behind him and watch for Syl's dust or his car. He was about halfway to Alpine when he missed Syl's car behind him. He pulled over to the side of the road and waited for Syl.

After about twenty minutes, Roy decided that something had happened. Roy turned his car around and headed back toward Marathon. He went a few miles and noticed Syl's car overturned in the pasture. This sight frightened Roy. He just knew he was going to find Syl dead. The car was a total wreck and there appeared to be nothing left. Roy brought his car to a screeching halt and jumped from it, expecting the worst.

After looking around the battered car, he noticed Syl propped up against the bent bumper of his car. There he sat with his drink of sotol in his hand. He glanced up at Roy, smiled, held up his drink, and nodded. "Didn't spill a drop, Roy!"

The two men gathered up their wits, shared a final drink, hopped in Roy's car, and headed to Alpine to report the accident. The story that was told on the streets was not that Syl had survived the accident; it was that Syl had managed to flip his car and salvage his most important asset, his drink of sotol.

Building a Nest

ONCE I had established myself as a friendly and accepted neighbor, I enjoyed my stays in town. I spent hours making our home in town one of which Roy would be proud. Between the ranch and the house in town, I seldom had time to relax. I always knew when we had been in town too long. Roy would let me know first with his restlessness and then with his hurried preparations for a return trip home.

I was more than glad to be going back home to the ranch after the confusion of the car race, the medicine show, and the drinking. It seemed to be the place where I belonged, the place of contentment and utter tranquility. There I could gaze at the mountains, watch the changing colors at sunset, and sit on a rock and listen to the various creatures of the land as they gathered their families together for the night. What a luxury it would be to be home.

As I returned home I swore that I would never forsake that ranch. The first thing I did was to seek out my favorite spot on the dune.

As I sat quietly on a rock, I thought of Papa and his love for the land. He said that land was a precious thing and that everyone should strive for land. *He* always did and always managed somehow to own land – sometimes large holdings and sometimes small acreage. Papa loved the land and he loved to grow things. I could remember his growing cotton at San Angelo, raising cows at the ranch between Fort Stockton and Sanderson, growing beans and potatoes on his farm in New Mexico, and raising goats and tending a garden at Lajitas in Fresno Canyon. At our home in Alpine, we always had a garden of vegetables and flowers. I did not inherit his knack of growing things, but I did inherit his love of land.

Having been in town for several days, Roy was anxious to look at the cattle and check the water tanks. He lost no time in letting me know what we needed to do.

"Saddle up, there's cow work to do," Roy called out, and we prepared to do the work that had been neglected while we were in town.

I was happy to be back in the saddle on the hills working by my husband's side along with Lee and Jona. We left Uncle Bob at the house, something we often did unless there was extra work. I depended on Uncle Bob to have our meals ready and do odd jobs around the house so I could ride with the men, something I really enjoyed. As I rode, I wondered if my pregnancy would be in jeopardy. I really knew very little about pregnancy since women were not well prepared for such things at that time. I wanted to continue working beside Roy, but I also wanted to protect my new baby.

One day I said to Roy, "Do you think it will hurt for me to ride horseback so much now that I'm pregnant?"

"You can do what you're used to doing and be all right," Roy explained to me. "Exercise is important, and you get your exercise on horseback."

I accepted Roy's word as law and continued to ride with the men until I could no longer find any pants that I could squeeze my stomach into. Then I had to accept my pregnancy as being a larger part of my life, much larger than my working next to Roy. I resigned myself to spending most of my days working around the house after that time. I could always find work that needed to be done, although I preferred riding.

Those days during my pregnancy were hot, but the months did pass quickly as I kept myself busy with ranch work and all the daily chores. I knew that my baby would soon be coming and that then I would have plenty to think about! Life would be full of new surprises.

Son Arrives

ALTHOUGH my pregnancy made me uncomfortable at times, I still enjoyed life at the ranch. Always early in the morning while Roy and the men tended to the horses and did other outside chores, I swept the dirt floor under the cool arbor and wet it down so that it would be a refreshing spot for the men when they came in from a day's work. I had planted vines so that there would be a shade around the arbor. It wasn't long before those honeysuckle vines prepared a shaded arbor, and we all enjoyed sitting outside in the afternoon and evenings.

It was 1919 and the middle of August when Roy decided that I should go to Marathon to stay until after our baby came. We had not consulted with the local doctor, G. W. Worthington, at any time during this pregnancy, so Roy was a little apprehensive. Since Marathon was such a small town, everyone knew everyone else's business. Most of the townspeople knew more about my delivery date than I did. Roy had been in town one day and came across Dr. Worthington at the post office and told him that we would be needing him shortly. Other than this conversation, we had made no contact with the doctor. Dr. Worthington was the typical country doctor. He owned a ranch and often spent weeks at a time there. Knowing this, Roy wanted to make sure that he would be around for my delivery, so he pushed me to town early.

I packed my belongings and the few baby things I had made and moved to town. It wasn't long before the men at the ranch and around town were making bets on the delivery date and sex of our baby. It appeared that the people in town were more concerned than I was about my baby. I was too busy hemming diapers and making little gowns and dresses for the baby. I sewed tatting on the dresses and even crocheted some on the hems. I thought that I had done well preparing the layette, and I had little time to worry about the baby's sex or date of birth.

As delivery time got closer, Roy became more worried. He said that I would have to have a maid to help me with the housework and the baby. He hired Rita, a Seminole Indian about fourteen years old. Rita was a wonderful helper, and once she came to work, she did everything for me. Even though she did not speak English, I knew some Spanish, her main language, so we managed to open a line of communication. She was quick to learn and soon was speaking English, at least enough to understand my directions and help me with my pregnancy. I very quickly began to depend on that wonderful girl.

67

I stepped into September hot and large. Movement was difficult and I did very little because of the heat and my size. On September 21, our first son was born. We were all very excited about the new baby and Roy was particularly happy about having a son, and from that day until today he has been called Son. Even though Son was his accepted name, we gave him the legal name of Roy Walker. His middle name came from Roy's good friend, Jim Walker, but our son knew his name only as Son Stillwell until he started to school. He was quite surprised to learn that he had a new name when school began.

Son's birth was not an easy one for me. He weighed twelve pounds and eight ounces. With only a country doctor and Rita, no anesthesia, and forty-eight hours of labor, I was pretty well exhausted when Son arrived. I had to stay in bed for eighteen days after his birth. Because of the difficult birth, Roy also hired a full-time nurse to help me. She stayed with me until I was able to move around with little trouble. Once she was gone, Rita and I had Son to ourselves and we both soon realized how little we knew about caring for an infant. I had to have more help, so I called on my sister Mabel.

She answered my call willingly and stayed with me until I was strong enough to handle things on my own. While Mabel was with me, she taught me how to cope with colic and the everyday infant problems that mothers experience. Once Mabel was secure that I knew what to do and she believed that I could manage with Rita, she returned to her home and family. I adjusted, but I really missed her and I think Rita did too.

Mother instinct helped me through the trying days of caring for Son. I had grown up as a tomboy, always doing outside chores and following around in my father's footsteps. I could milk a cow, harness a team of horses to a wagon, manipulate a turning plow, carry stove wood and water, and kill a deer for meat and hides. But I knew very little about domestic living. I had always left household chores to Mabel. She had always been like a mother, helping with the younger children, cooking, and cleaning house. Mabel had cared for Alvin, Lovenia, and Glen when they were small. These siblings had always turned to Mabel whenever they needed comfort and couldn't get it from Mama, who was so often busy around the house. Even my older brother Frank was a better help in the house to Mama than I ever was. I just had never had an interest in the home life, so being a mother was a completely foreign experience for me.

In spite of my ignorance of motherhood, Son thrived on my love, which deepened as the days flew by. Roy was very proud of his son, and I soon found that I had to take a backseat to Roy's attention as his love for Son grew in intensity. Once I realized this, I knew that our family was complete.

Son was about two months old before we took him on his first trip to the ranch. The weather was cold that winter and I stayed in town most of the time, but I soon longed for the mountains, cacti, and my dune. The trip was easy but short. Roy didn't want us to stay long because of the cold, and we returned to town, where we spent most of that winter. I spent most of my days playing with or caring for Son, but occasionally I would pull myself away from the baby and visit neighbors or play a few hands of bridge. I enjoyed the outings but was always glad to get back to the baby. Because I was forced to stay in town along with Rita and the baby, I had no choice but to learn all I could about motherhood that winter, and it became a joy in my life.

Spring budded in early April and Rita and I were anxious to get back to the ranch. We gathered up Son and our collection of baby clothes and supplies and moved ourselves back to the ranch. I was truly excited about getting home, being with Roy once again, and getting reacquainted with the men. I could hardly wait to see their faces when I showed them Son.

I was somewhat surprised at the reactions of the men to Son. They were more excited about the baby than they were over the birthing of a newborn calf. I did expect them to notice Son, but I got much more than I expected. Once we were settled in at the ranch, Son became the center of attention. We had added a new member to the family.

Because I had Rita, I was able to return to my work with Roy and the men. I was "back in the saddle again" and I loved it. I felt that my life was complete: husband, baby, family, and friends. I often wondered what more I could want. Needless to say, there is always more – some good, some bad.

Spanish Influenza Strikes

As I mentioned before, Lucius and Margaret Buttrill were our good friends and neighbors. Roy had known Margaret since she was a little girl and had known Lucius since he came to the Big Bend country in 1884 from Beeville. Their friendship with Roy began many years before I had made my entry into the Marathon area.

Margaret was a friendly, outgoing person with a heart as big as a mountain. She had married Lou Buttrill, a man much older than she, and had lived through many years as a pioneer ranchman's wife and devoted mother of two lovely daughters, Marion and Louanna. Since Marion and I were the same age, Margaret became like a mother to me.

Lou was a hardworking and honest man who was a good husband, father, and ranchman. He was admired by all who knew him and was often referred to as a man among men.

The Buttrills had been ranching on a large spread in the Rosillas Mountains. However, when the Pancho Villa raiders and the troubled Mexican situation had caused serious problems, Lou had moved his family to Marathon for safety. He then prepared to establish a ranch away from the troubled border country. He purchased land some fifteen miles south of Marathon and built a beautiful ranch home there for his family. It was at this home, which was so conveniently located on the road to our ranch, that I had the great opportunity to get to know and love the entire Buttrill family.

Roy and I had been at our ranch for a week or so when he came in and announced that we had better go back to town because Christmas was soon to come. That was good news to me, so I wasted no time in gathering up my baby and Rita, the maid. We were ready shortly to pull out for town.

On our way into town, we stopped by the Buttrill Ranch as we usually did and visited the family. Margaret had prepared a good dinner, and Roy and I were delighted to stay and share their food. Margaret was known as one of the best cooks in the area, and I did not disagree. She was a perfect hostess and we always felt welcome, day or night. Lou in his quiet way was proud of Margaret and enjoyed sharing her company and their home.

After we had eaten and retired to comfortable chairs in front of the beautiful rock fireplace, Roy and Lou talked over the ranching business and the conditions of the country. Margaret and I continued with our women's talk and tended to Son while Rita and Margaret's maid, Otelia (Rita's sister), washed the dinner dishes. Later that evening, after a wonderful visit, Roy and I gathered up Son and Rita and left for town.

As we drove along, Roy said, "Lou and I are going to buy some steers and pasture them at our ranch on the shares."

"Is that what you and Lou were talking about while Margaret and I were visiting?"

"Yes!" exclaimed Roy. "Lou sold his Rosillas Ranch and has some extra money to invest. He'll put up the money and I'll furnish the pasture, and we'll split the profit."

"Sounds like a good deal to me," I said.

"Lou says that he'll go to New Mexico and buy some steers up there."

Everything appeared cut and dried to me.

A few weeks later, Margaret came to stay with us in town while Lou made the trip to New Mexico to get the steers. In a few days, Margaret became ill with the Spanish influenza and was not able to get out of bed. I called Dr. Worthington and he did what he could. The disease was so new that doctors did not know how to treat it successfully, so they usually had to experiment on each patient. Dr. Worthington told me that there would probably be an epidemic of the influenza and that it would probably hit Marathon along with all the other parts of our nation. We had heard that soldier boys in the army camps were taken down with the disease and there was not enough knowledge and medicine to care for them properly. Again it came to mind that my own brother, Frank, was one of the first victims of this dreaded disease. His bout with it had been followed by pneumonia and then, shortly, death.

Margaret recovered from the influenza while in town and was well enough to return to her ranch when Lou returned from New Mexico with the herd of steers. We decided that I would go home with her while Roy took the steers to the ranch. I was happy to visit Margaret and stay on their ranch. I quickly packed my belongings and Son's and in a short time we were ready.

As we loaded up to head for the Buttrill Ranch, Roy began to drive the herd of steers to our ranch. I had told Rita to gather her things and go with us so that she could help with Son. Rita was more than glad to go to the Buttrill Ranch because she could visit with her sister Otelia.

The first night I spent at that ranch, I awakened at midnight feeling very ill. I knew at once that I had been taken with the dreaded influenza. I tossed and turned and worried all night long. As the night continued, I became more ill. When Margaret came into my room the next morning to wake me for breakfast, she found me in tears.

"Oh, Margaret, I'm so sick. I have the influenza. What will I do?" I cried.

Margaret did not bat an eye. She came over to my bed, looked straight into my red, tear-stained face, and said, "Shut up that bawling. I'm going to take care of you. Give me that baby!" At that, Margaret left the room.

That really angered me! I was so upset that I could have fought a circle of saws. I pulled the covers up over my head, gritted my teeth, and vowed that I would not be ill. I told myself that I did not have the influenza. I thought to myself, "I'll show Margaret!"

I decided to get out of my bed. I fully intended to get my baby and tend to him myself. I was not going to be a crybaby. Just as I was attempting to raise my head from my pillow, a hard chill came over me, and I was forced to lie back down and pull more covers over my shaking body.

As I lay in that bed, these thoughts surfaced: "Where are my friends, where are those who care for me, where is Roy, where is my baby?" As my thoughts began to clear, I felt my courage returning and I once again vowed to fight to the finish and thought of other times when I had to fight to live.

When I was three years old, my family was living in Ozona. I came down with a severe case of typhoid fever that was followed by pneumonia. I was at death's door for several days. At one time during that critical period, Dr. Clayton (our physician at the time) sat by my bedside for twenty-four hours. I believe that he pulled me back to life. He later told others that I had fought for life with the courage of a lion.

When I was seven years old and my family was living in San Angelo, I was stricken with the dreaded disease diphtheria. I came down with the only known case in that city at that time. My mother was in a state of panic and thought that the disease was always fatal. Our doctor assured her that a new serum had just been discovered and was successful in treating it. I was given the dosage. With the serum and my youth as an advantage, I once again recovered. The red flag of quarantine that had waved on our porch is a picture that I shall never forget.

With such thoughts running through my mind and seeing myself a victim of such a dreaded illness, I braced myself and gathered up all the courage that I was able to muster. I was determined to fight the call of death once more.

"Here you are and looking much better!" said Margaret as she smilingly handed me a cup of hot coffee. "Lou has gone to town to bring Dr. Worthington to see you, and Rita has fed Son and dressed him while you've been sick. Son is asleep now on the couch in the living room. I know that you're worried about coming down with this influenza, but don't worry, we're going to take good care of you. You'll be fine. I've sent word to Roy to come and you just need to relax, stay covered up, and let me wait on you."

As she finished her report, she walked over to my bed, felt my brow as she pushed my hair from my face, fluffed up the pillow, and said, "Just call me if you want anything. I'll be in the kitchen and will hear you call."

As I awoke from a feverish stupor, Dr. Worthington was standing over me with his thermometer. I showed a fever of 104 degrees and there was a look on his face that I had the dreaded disease, and I knew that he did not know any more about it than other doctors across the country. His instructions were simple. "Take aspirin and quinine, drink liquids, and keep covered up." He told Margaret to keep the baby away from me.

As he left my bedside he said, "I'll be back tomorrow." Margaret said he had to rush to visit another patient who had the same thing.

Roy arrived at the ranch late that afternoon. Margaret soon discovered that Roy was also sick with the influenza. She quickly put him to bed in the "twin" room (Louanna and Marion's rooms were connected by a large double door) next to mine. Margaret told Roy that I was too ill to be bothered and that he needed to start taking the medicine that I had been given. Roy was too sick to argue, and he surrendered himself to the care of the Buttrills.

The next day Rita too came down with the influenza, so Margaret sent to Marathon for assistance. (The hired hands on the Buttrill's ranch had also come down with the influenza, leaving her with no one to help her.) But Mary, Rita's cousin, who came from Marathon to assist Margaret, also soon came down with the illness. Next came Bitana, Mary's sister, who also quickly fell ill. Margaret then sent to Alpine. Mrs. Curtley, a friend of Margaret's and an acquaintance of mine, came to help with Son and a trained nurse was sent to take care of the ill. During that time, Margaret certainly had her hands full!

Roy recovered much faster than I. My fever stayed at 104 degrees for eight days, and Dr. Worthington came every day to see me even though he had a town full of sick people. It was no little chore for him to come the sixteen miles over dirt roads in a jitney (a small Ford car). I will be forever grateful for his kind attention.

Margaret and Lou never faltered. They kept after all the ranch work and the chores involved in keeping the household intact. It was their constant care of us that aided in our recovery. Of all the people who fell ill on the Buttrill's ranch, only one elderly woman died from the illness. In Alpine and Marathon, several of our close friends died during this epidemic, including Roy's nephew, John Henderson. John was a close family relation who worked with Roy in many business dealings. He and Roy worked cattle together and Roy thought that he was one of the best bronc riders in the country. Roy depended on him whenever help was needed. Because of the close ties between Roy and John, John's death was a hard blow to us. We were not told of his death until after we were well and ready to go to our own home. That news really made our trip home a silent one.

The outbreak of the Spanish influenza was a tragedy of the times. Schools were closed, public meetings were banned, and business was limited to only a few customers in a building at one time. Brewster County as well as other surrounding places had more influenza victims than war-related casualties.

By the time my fever broke, Roy was much improved and anxious to be going home to the ranch. Dr. Worthington cautioned us to take our time and not rush things. He said to me, "You're fortunate to be on the road to recovery."

After a few more days, we said goodbye to Margaret and Lou and to the nurse and Mrs. Curtly. I knew that I would feel lost without them and that the adjustment ahead of me would be a challenge.

Rita had also recovered from the influenza and was anxious to be back to help me. I welcomed her with open arms and we cried together over the past weeks' events. Too much had happened to our friends and relatives during the epidemic, and we both knew that we were feeling like the lucky ones.

After being cooped up and ill for several days, Roy was "chomping at the bit" to get back home. I was still weak and unable to do all the things necessary for a move to our ranch; however, with Rita's help, we managed and were soon on our way.

Lee and Jona had tended the new steers while Roy was away. They were glad to see us return and had many details to report to Roy. They talked as if they had not seen another human being for days, and Roy listened attentively. Soon they were all ready to saddle up and ride off. Rita and I watched as they rode away from the house, and we surveyed our situation as we prepared for the days to come.

Roy and the men had enlarged our arbor before we all became ill. They had put a layer of candelilla on the top of it to make a good shade. I loved that arbor, and once again I planted my beloved vines of honeysuckle. Those vines helped to make a better shade, and I was very proud of my addition to our home. I soon made that arbor my living room.

It wasn't long before Rita and I had the ranch home in order. There was really not much to do since we only had bare necessities to deal with. Our daily chores of cleaning the coal oil lamp chimneys, filling the lamps, using a broom to sweep sand off the floors, and making up beds were the extent of our housework. The cooking was simple as we only had certain things to fix, and if we were out of something, we were just out. There were no convenient stores or any places to buy supplies close by. We just learned to manage with what we had when we had it.

Son was healthy and growing like wildfire. He attracted the attention of Lee, Jona, and Uncle Bob. They enjoyed entertaining him and it often appeared as though Son was the only one on the ranch. Life was settling back to normal.

Early one morning Roy asked me, "Are you ready to ride all day? We're short-handed and need you to help us. Rita can care for Son, and we'll be back before dark.

I hesitated momentarily about leaving my baby for such a long period of time, but knew that he would be in good hands, so I told Roy that I would go with him. Rita didn't like the idea of being left alone at the ranch without me. Fortunately, I had taught her to use a gun and thinking of this, I cautioned her carefully.

"Now, Rita, there's a loaded gun in every corner of this house. If anyone comes around who looks suspicious, use a gun." I reminded her what Roy had taught me. He had always said not to let a stranger come to the door and always have him stop at the gate. I quoted his words: "If you let anyone get any closer, it will be too late."

Rita listened with her eyes wide and her expression fearful as I continued to caution her. "Remember what Roy says, 'shoot to kill – never to scare.'" I thought of Rita being a Seminole Indian and felt somewhat better. I knew that she would stand her ground and protect my son with her life if necessary. I had little fear in leaving Son with her. I walked away feeling secure.

As I recovered and days passed, I rode more with Roy and the cowboys. At that time, our biggest concern became the anticipation and need of rain. Bluebonnets had begun to bloom along with several other types of wildflowers. Every day brought new wonders of growing plants, and I saw the country in a glory that I had never seen before. It was a whole new world that unfolded before my eyes. All around me were the beauty of the flowers, the cuteness of newborn calves, and the symphony of the birds in the trees and cacti. All of these wonders bore a special meaning to me, and I felt that I was blessed by all the wonders of West Texas. I was loving the ranchland more and more as the days passed quickly. With all that I had, I then felt that I was a part of the ranch and Roy's life forever.

California

Since Roy and I had recovered from the influenza, Mama and Papa were anxious for us to come to Phoenix for a visit. They wanted to see their first grandson. I felt some homesickness for my parents and wanted to show off our new baby. I was reluctant to mention these feelings to Roy, though. I kept them bottled up inside me for some time.

One day as Roy was resting after a good dinner, I approached the subject of taking a trip. "Now that the ranch work is caught up, do you think we could visit Mama and Papa? We could even go on to California and visit your sister Lizzie."

I expected a negative answer and was surprised that Roy seemed pleased with the idea. He responded with words I did not expect to hear from him. "Now is a good time to go. Can you get Son and us ready to travel in a week?"

I jumped up and answered joyfully, "I sure can!"

In preparation for the trip, Roy sold his beautiful Hudson Super-6 roadster and bought a new Essex. This car had a top, something we needed when we traveled as a family. It even had a set of curtains that snapped on to use in rainy and cold weather.

I was so excited that I had us packed and ready in no time. We were soon on our way. We stopped in Alpine and asked my friend Eugenia Dantzler if she wanted to make the trip with us. We told her that she could visit her aunt, who was living in Mariposa, which was just outside Phoenix.

She quickly accepted our invitation and was ready to load up very shortly. After we left Alpine, we drove straight to El Paso where we stopped, shopped, toured Juarez Mexico, and did some sightseeing. After enjoying two days in El Paso, we headed for Wilcox, Arizona. There we stopped and visited friends and attended a two-day celebration in honor of Independence Day. We enjoyed horse racing, a rodeo, and dancing at night.

After a few days in Wilcox, we stopped next in Mariposa, where we left Eugenia. By that time, we were anxious to reach Phoenix. We stopped seldom after that. Our sights were set for Mama and Papa.

Outside of El Paso, I had seen no large cities. I was overwhelmed with Phoenix and its wide city streets, huge buildings, and beauty. We had to drive to Uncle Jim Crawford's house to find out where Mama and Papa were living. My brother Alvin was living with the Crawfords and working in Phoenix. I was excited to find that Alvin had discovered a young girl, Doris. She was the girl next door to the Crawfords and Alvin was in love, but Doris did not know this. Alvin told me all about his dreams and explained that he was only a working man and could provide her with few fine things. He did so want to impress her.

After listening to Alvin, I approached Roy. "Roy, do you think you might let Alvin borrow our car tonight? He has a date with the next-door neighbor girl and would like to show her a good time."

Roy smiled and handed me the keys to the car. Was Alvin ever excited! I knew from the look on his face that he could not have been more pleased if he had just bought the car himself. I'm not sure whether the car had anything to do with that love affair but not long after our trip, Alvin and Doris were married.

The next day, after getting directions from Uncle Jim, we loaded up once more and headed for the outskirts of Phoenix, where Mama and Papa were living. We drove up a road lined with beautiful poppies in full bloom. As we stopped in front of their farmhouse, they met us at the gate. They could hardly believe the size of Son and thought that he was the finest baby boy ever born. We visited with Mama and Papa for a week and then gathered up our "duds" and headed for California. The days were hot, a heat that I almost could not stand. I worried about Son constantly, wondering if the heat was too much for him. There were times when the hot sand seemed to jump at us, but we pushed on. In some of the sandy places, a board roadway was laid, which helped considerably. At least, we did not feel the tremendous heat from the sand so closely. We had never seen boards used a roadways, but we were certainly glad they were there.

The crossing of the Colorado River on a barge was a new experience for me. It turned out to be a frightening one too. The river was at flood stage with all kinds of logs, trees, and trash rolling in its swift currents. We were the only car loaded to cross, and I expected the sputtering engine on the barge to stop at any minute. However, it chugged along and we arrived on the other bank safely and soundly. Once my feet touched the ground, I told Roy rather emphatically, "I never want to do that again!"

We finally arrived at Long Beach, where Roy's sister lived. She was happy to have us come, and she went to all kinds of trouble to make us feel welcome and happy. She knew that it was my first trip to the oceanfront and she took us sightseeing, to museums, libraries, art galleries, and we even saw the oldest grapevine in the country. She refused to let us miss a single sight. By the time we had seen everything, I was worn to a frazzle. Although I appreciated all that Lizzie had done for us, and I enjoyed all the sights, I was glad when we said our good-byes and started back toward Texas.

We drove as far as Barstow, California, and Roy put Son and me on the train headed for El Paso. He did not want the baby and me to have to endure the long hot trip back through the desert. I really did not mind the trip over the desert as much as I dreaded the thought of getting on that barge again. Roy must have felt my apprehension, and he quickly made my life much easier with his decision.

When I arrived in El Paso, Son and I hailed a cab and stationed ourselves at the Shelton Hotel, where we waited for Roy. It was not a long wait. Roy came into the hotel raring to go home. I was as anxious as he was. It didn't take us long to load our gear and bound for the ranch.

We only stopped in Marathon for a short while and then continued on to the ranch. We reached home in the evening and were met by the men. We had many tales to tell Lee, Jona, and Uncle Bob. I realized that as I told my experiences, I continually repeated the same words over and over, "I don't like the ocean. The waves constantly moving in and out are more than I can take." Funny how I remembered visualizing the Pacific Ocean as being peaceful and magnificent. The closer I got to the ocean, the more exciting and suspenseful it became. Boy, was I surprised. I told Jona, "I watched the constant waves hitting against the land, and I felt that if just one wave would stay back, I could endure the repeated splashing and pounding, but they never stopped."

Lee asked, "How was the beach?"

"It was too sandy for me and there were too many people lying around in and on the sand. Those people were barely dressed and most of them were getting sunburned." I realized that the beach held no appeal for me any longer.

I did speak of the beautiful flowers, the large orange groves, and the lush vegetation in California. I also enjoyed the museums, libraries, and other facets of the state that we saw. I did make up my mind that I never wanted to live there.

As I mulled over the entire trip, I decided that the worst part of our trip was the short visit with Mama and Papa. I hated to leave them in Arizona knowing that they were "true Texans" at heart. I remember thinking about leaving them. Papa gave me a sense that he had made a mistake, that they were out of place in Arizona. I did not sense the homey atmosphere in their house, the feeling I always experienced when I entered their home in Alpine. The people in Arizona were much different from Mama and Papa. They acted differently, spoke strangely, and even had ideas that appeared strange to most Texans. In reality, Mama and Papa were just not in Texas where they should have been.

That night as Roy and I lay in bed, I told him that I would not be happy until my parents returned to Texas. I guess I was feeling the pains of adulthood; I was worrying about my parents and wanting to take care of them. They had spent so many years caring for me and my welfare, and suddenly I was seeing them through the same caring eyes with which they had watched me so closely. I realized then that they needed me as much as I needed them.

Dadie

LIVING with Roy had taught me never to ask questions – just bide my time and all would unfold. Lee brought in the remuda from Dove Mountain and the shoeing of horses began. I knew that meant the fall work was in the making. I watched with interest as saddles and bridles were greased and repaired and even the saddle blankets were washed and hung out to dry in the sun.

I was surprised when a strange Mexican man and his two sons came with six burros and set up camp out in back of the sand pile. My curiosity was getting the best of me and I mustered up the courage to ask Roy, "What are all those wet Mexicans and burros going to do here?"

"They'll cut Chino grass that grows in the mountains and bring it in to build a haystack. This will give us Chino hay for our saddle horses all winter," Roy replied.

"Will you also be buying oats for the horses?" I asked.

"No, the Chino is very strong. You can ride a horse harder and longer if he's fed on Chino grass instead of oats."

I watched as the Mexicans set up their camp, which only took about fifteen minutes. Early the next morning the men fashioned pack saddles from wood that would fit over the backs of the burros. These pack saddles were bound with scrap leather that was found around the house; they would carry the bundles of Chino grass. Next, the men gathered their burros and headed for the high mountain country to collect the grass. I watched until they were out of sight.

I didn't know that anything was better than oats for horses, but I was learning. That evening I watched with interest as the men brought the burros from the mountain loaded from head to tail with bundles

11. Mexican man with load of chino grass, 1920

of Chino grass. Each burro looked like one huge bundle as he carefully crept along the winding trail that led down the mountain. Soon
the haystack began to take shape as bundle after bundle of Chino grass
was put in place. When Roy saw that there was enough of the grass
to last through the winter, he let the old man and his boys grub (cut)
brush and trees out of a good lowland spot to make a field.

Roy and I had just been married about two years at this time and
I found out that I was pregnant again. I really hadn't wanted to be
pregnant so soon after Son's birth, as he was still in diapers. I didn't
relish the idea of giving birth to another child weighing over twelve
pounds, either. I had been feeling fine, riding horses, and being a cowhand on the ranch as usual. I did not even want to take a day off to
have another baby, and I often wondered how Roy would react to
this surprising news.

There were several days when I started to tell Roy about the new
baby, but then I would lose my courage. I managed through most of
the fall and the beginning of winter before I decided to spring the news
on Roy. It was either tell him or come up with some explanation for
my excessive gain in weight.

On Christmas Day, I mustered up my wits and bravery. I walked up to Roy after Christmas dinner, looked him right in the eye, and said, "I'm going to have another baby."

Roy just stared at me for a few seconds. I knew he was letting my remark soak in, and I wasn't anticipating the best of answers. I knew that he needed me more on the range than in the house giving birth. But once again he surprised me. He suddenly blurted out, "That's great. I want a big family. When do you expect this one?"

I wasn't sure how to take his response, so I just looked at him and mumbled, "In June, I think." I was completely overwhelmed with my new pregnancy – and with Roy.

After the initial shock of being pregnant again, things settled right back into the usual routine. Even though I was carrying another child, ranch work continued as usual. Nothing really changed.

During the month of December, I watched as the Mexican man and his sons cleared a field near the house; I wondered what Roy was up to. Once again I gathered my courage and asked Roy if he intended to do a little farming.

"I'm going to raise some corn, maize, and cane to feed our chickens and a milk cow." At that point I reminded Roy that I was never going to raise chickens or have a milk cow.

Roy ignored my remark and stated, "We'll plow next spring and then plant." Roy said that he wanted to grow things and he wanted a garden and grapevines. I thought these remarks strange coming from the cowman I had married. I had always thought that he was only interested in horses and cows. During those days it was uncommon for a ranchman to plant anything, and certainly farmers did not usually ride ranges, brand, or work cattle. I was seeing a side of Roy that was somewhat different than the image he had earlier conveyed. As I listened to Roy, I immediately thought of Lou Buttrill and his wonderful ranch house that was surrounded by gardens, fruit trees, and grapevines. Then Charley and Tom Green, our close neighbors to the west, came to mind. Those men had a wonderful peach orchard and a garden that produced the greatest vegetables and best watermelons in West Texas. I began to think how wonderful it would be to have fresh vegetables and fruit and was glad that Roy was interested in trying his hand at planting.

The old Mexican man and his two sons were quite content and worked steadily at clearing a fifteen-acre field. At night we would hear those men talking even as we drifted off to sleep. When we would wake in the mornings, those Mexicans would still be talking. That went on all winter. Finally I asked Roy, "What do you suppose they're talking about? They haven't seen anyone, just themselves, and have no outside contacts at all."

Roy answered, "Absolutely nothing. They just talk and talk and talk – never saying anything."

Roy kept the men until they finished clearing the fields and sent them back to Mexico some time in February. Roy told me that he and I would hitch up the mules and plant the seeds ourselves. I was anxious to get the corn seed in the ground so I could see the results of our winter work.

Ranch work went along as usual, with the winter days passing quickly. By the end of February Roy had decided it was time to plant our newly cleared fields. Lee and Jona were over at Dove Mountain working. Uncle Bob and Rita took care of Son while Roy and I began to get things ready to plant. We first hitched up our two mules to a plow. Then, we gathered up the corn seed and headed for the fields.

I knew much more about plowing than Roy did and together we mastered the art. I drove the mules while Roy held the plow. I had tried to guide the plow while Roy drove the mules but I could never seem to get straight furrows. Roy would yell, "Lift up on those handles!" I would and the plow would go directly into the ground. Then Roy would yell, "Bear down!" I would and the plow would come up out of the ground. I created a real mess and finally gave up. Roy quickly put me back to driving the mules. Roy and I worked several weeks on that field and our bodies told us that we had really worked hard. When we finished, our feet were sore and our backs weary. I think that was about the hardest work we ever did. Roy was a good worker on horseback, could ride harder and farther than anyone in the country, but on foot he was not worth a tinker's dam. Our hard efforts paid off, though. The rains came at the right time and our first crop was a bumper crop, one that we were very proud of. We even had so much corn that we had plenty to share with our neighbors. Because of the success of our farming, we viewed ranching from a different angle than we had in the past.

Spring came with beautiful warmth, but as June arrived the days became hot. I was very uncomfortable and anxious for my baby to come since I had to remain around the house all day. I was delighted to get a letter from Mama telling me that she would come to be with me while I had the baby. I was glad to get into town and get settled for the occasion. With a joyous heart I met the train that brought Mama to me.

On June 18 my baby daughter was born. Son was glad to see the baby and would stand over her time and again saying, "Dadie, Dadie." He could not say the word *baby*. We named her Elizabeth Marie; however, she has never been known by any name other than Dadie to this day. With Son not yet two years old and a newborn to care for, it was heartwarming to have Mama there. I wished that she could have stayed forever, but she had her duties at home with Papa and my younger sisters, Lovenia and Glen. After a two-week stay with me, she returned to Phoenix. I really missed her loving care and help. I felt my responsibilities more and more. I turned to Rita, my dear Rita, for consolation and help. She was always there for me.

Roy loved the two babies. He was overjoyed with their presence and while he could care for a baby calf or a newborn animal of any kind, he could not change a baby's diaper or rock one to sleep. I was glad to have Roy leave his ranch duties to Lee and Jona and come into town to be with me. He was handy with the shopping and cooking, and I loved the attention he gave the babies and me. Roy helped make having children a wonderful experience.

Roy and I decided that it would be best for me to stay in town all summer, since the hot days would be hard for the babies and me. I missed being at home in the country and as soon as cool weather came, I headed for the ranch and Roy.

While I was in town with the babies I was asked to join the bridge club, which I did. I loved going to the bridge parties. Roy and I also took in the Fourth of July celebration at the Post. (Fort Pena Colorado, then and now called the Post, was where celebrations like this were held.) There was a noon barbecue, after which a dance platform was erected under a big cottonwood tree. Shortly thereafter, Mexican music and dancing began and lasted until the wee morning hours. There were also goat ropings and horse racing – and something for everyone.

The Post had once been the site of an army camp. Nearby were some rock houses where men were quartered and some rock pens where their horses were kept. Near the pens was a parade ground. Early soldiers had planted trees along the Maravillas Creek bank. They also used a large dugout area of the creek for a bathing and swimming hole.

The first ranch families of Marathon settled at the Post and lived there until the Southern Pacific Railroad was built some five miles north. Naturally everyone left the Post and settled near the Southern Pacific Railroad, where Marathon is today. The land where the Post is situ-

12. Dove Mountain shacks, 1928; Dadie is in front of buildings

ated belonged to the Combs Cattle Company. In later years, Guy Combs, manager and owner of this large ranching company, gave this land to Brewster County to be used as a recreation park to be enjoyed by all. Shortly after this donation, Margaret Buttrill, Tom Yarbro, and I were appointed by the Brewster County Commissioner's Court as trustees of this park. As trustees, we were responsible for keeping up the grounds as well as improving them. A flood came one year and the Maravillas Creek flowed heavily over its banks. The flood caused many of those huge, beautiful cottonwood trees to be washed down the creek. That left the area barren. Only a few of the original cotton-woods were left standing. We trustees ordered pecan trees and planted them along the banks to replace the destroyed cottonwoods. Also, during the depression of the thirties, the trustees had the WPA (Works Projects Administration) workers build a dam across the creek and a swimming pool on one side. This park is still used and enjoyed by many today.

The year Dadie was born had been an extremely dry one and the lack of rain was depressing to all ranchers. By May, most of the ranch-men were having a hard time. Cattle were losing weight and surface tanks were getting low and very boggy. When a tank became boggy cattle would often get stuck in the mud and would either die or have to be pulled out. Every rancher was busy trying to keep his herds supplied with grass and water.

A ranchman in the Chisos Mountains had run a herd of twelve hundred Mexican steers on his ranch all year but was forced to ship them out because of the dry weather. He gathered his steers and started to Marathon with them where they would be loaded onto the train. They had to stop at Double Mills, some thirty-two miles from Marathon, to spend the night. The steers were watered and settled down for the night. The cowboys were tired after being on the trail for three days, so they thought a good night's rest was a good idea.

Far into the quiet night a strong east wind came up, suddenly causing the steers to stampede. By the time the cowboys could mount their horses, the herd had disappeared into the darkness of the night. For two days those cowboys looked for the steers with no luck in finding even a track to hint at where they had gone.

John Burris, who was in charge of the drive, was frantic. He was responsible for the delivery of the cattle. He happened to know Lou Buttrill, our neighbor, so he asked Lou if he knew anyone who would know how to find the lost herd.

Lou told him, "Yes, the only person who knows about Mexican cattle is Roy Stillwell. He can find them."

John and Lou hastened to see Roy and explained the situation. Roy responded that his own ranch problems were desperate and that he could not neglect his own cattle. He told the men he even had a sick wife with a new baby. (By this time we were both back at the ranch with Son and Dadie.)

Burris told Roy that he would furnish men to look after his ranch needs and that Margaret Buttrill and his own wife would look after me. Burris insisted "I have to find those lost steers!"

I could have killed Roy when he invited the Burrises and Buttrills into the ranch house to see me. Never in my whole life had I been more embarrassed. I had been sick in bed for a solid week with a boil on my chin. My lower lip was so swollen that it touched the end of my nose. My fever had been very high and I could not eat. I looked awful, the bed was in a tumble, and Dadie stayed by my side all day long depending on me for her needs. She was old enough to sit alone and there was no other place for her to be so that I could watch her. Everything around me was in a mess, and I felt helpless.

Roy had done the best he could for us. He was deeply concerned about my pain and had even taken his razor and lanced the boil, hoping that I would get better, but his cure didn't work.

I didn't mind so much for Margaret Buttrill to see me in that predicament, but Mrs. Burris (Bebe) was a stranger. Both women were nicely dressed, stylish and beautiful. I could have crawled into a badger hole as they sat and visited with me. But after a while I settled down and enjoyed their company. I realized that women talk was what I had needed.

Finally Roy agreed to do what he could to help John when he was convinced that I and the ranch would be in good hands. Roy remembered that on the night of the stampede there had been a strong east wind. He knew that Mexican steers would head into that wind. Roy saddled his horse and headed east. He came to where the cattle were last seen and cut for sign (rode in a cross-direction for signs). It was not long before Roy found tracks and he knew then that the steers would be found on the highest mountain they could find. With the help of John's cowboys, the men found all twelve hundred steers resting under a bluff on Cupolo Mountain, the highest in the area. The entire herd of steers were soon on the way to town escorted by happy cowboys. Fortunately, the cowboys had no more trouble.

It was not by a miracle or luck that Roy found the herd of stampeded Mexican steers. It was the fact that he knew from early life experiences the nature of those Mexican cattle. Because of Roy's knowledge, many ranchmen came to Roy for help with their herds or ranch problems.

That particular year brought many changes and excitement into our lives, along with hard times. Not only did we have a new baby daughter, but we had become successful farmers in a small way and were able to help our good neighbors. As the years progressed my life continued to improve.

Guy Is Born

1922 was a fairly normal year. There were few hardships on the ranch and our lives were spent keeping the ranch running smoothly.

Having two babies to tend caused the time to pass quickly. Before I knew it, Dadie was a year old and Son was following after Roy and the men. I spent most of my days helping Roy, working around the house, or caring for our two children. I had little time to fret or worry.

On the ranch days passed quickly as checking the herd for screwworms and repairing fences and windmills continued throughout the hot weather. It always seemed that there was no end to ranch work.

Nevertheless, Roy and I took time out to attend the annual fourth of July celebration at the Post. We enjoyed the barbecue and visits with neighbors and friends. In the afternoon, for entertainment, a horse race was held. The racehorses were local ponies that were thought to be extra-swift. Roy, being an expert rider, was always chosen as one of the jockeys. All the men were interested in the racing and enjoyed placing their money on their favorite horses. Those horse races were more for fun than for the bets made. Being a winner or loser was not so important to Roy; it was the race he enjoyed the most. That part of the celebration was one of Roy's favorites because he always loved riding a fast horse. The race was always followed by dancing to music played by a Mexican band. The celebration would continue into the early morning hours, bringing to a close a joyous day.

As summer came to an end, and again I saw the geese flying south in their beautiful V-formations, I knew that cold weather would soon come. We would shortly have to begin preparations for Christmas and the New Year. I loved the fun times of the holidays. On these special occasions, we would forget our ranch duties and join our friends in all the holiday activities in Marathon. Just after Christmas I was invited to a bridge party in Marathon, one I really wanted to attend. We had already returned to the ranch, but I stressed to Roy that I would really like to go.

Roy allowed me to drive to Marathon in our car, an Essex at that time. I loaded up Son and Dadie and we took off for Marathon early one morning. Everything was going well until I had a flat about twenty-five miles from the ranch. Few people traveled that road so I knew that I had to fix it myself. I knew what to do but had trouble with every aspect of that tire change, especially because I had to work in a dress. I learned from this one experience that I should never wear a dress but always wear pants when traveling alone. The bolts were rusted and I had to hammer and pound on them for some time before I could get them off. Once I loosened the bolts, I had trouble with the jack. The sun was beating down on me and the children were getting cranky. Just as I got the spare tire on the wheel, Louis Granger, an area rancher, drove up and asked if I needed any help. I quickly answered, "No, I'm okay now, but I sure wish you had come along sooner. I really could have used your help." I thanked him, loaded up the kids, and started on my journey once again as Louis headed in the other direction.

Some one hundred yards from where I had my first flat, I felt the car bump along the road. I knew immediately that I had another flat.

There I stood wondering if I would ever make the party. I unloaded the jack, the first tire, the patch kit, and Son and Dadie. I had to get the wheel off the axle, take the tire from the rim (a task no more easy for me than climbing a mountain), place a patch on the tube, pump up the tube, and remount the tube and tire before I could place the wheel back on the axle. The kids were unhappy and all I could do to entertain Dadie was to allow her to sit in the middle of the road and play in the rocks. At one point Son yelled at me, "Mama, Dadie eating rocks!"

My snappy response was: "Just let her eat them!"

That was one time when I wished I had not allowed Rita to leave the ranch and visit her family. I really needed her then, especially for my children. I was so frustrated that I could not think clearly about my situation or my children.

After several hours I finally had the tire on the axle and was headed once again to Marathon. I was so exhausted and distressed that I stopped at the Buttrills' house. As I pulled into the front gate of their house, Mr. and Mrs. Buttrill came out to greet me. They took one look at me, grabbed the children, left me alone in the car, and returned to the house. They never said a word.

I sat in that car for thirty minutes before I could pull myself together. I always appreciated their intuitiveness. They knew that I needed to be alone and they just took the children and left me sitting there. When I finally went into the house, they greeted me and listened to my story, fed us, and put us to bed. I had not intended to spend the night, but the party was not until the next day, so I was glad for their hospitality.

After a good night's rest, the children and I left early the next morning. I had really wanted to attend that party, and I did. The trip from the Buttrills' to Marathon was uneventful, something that I was very thankful for. I left Son and Dadie at the house with Rita and made the party with sore muscles, scratched and swollen hands, lots of lost skin, and a wounded pride, but I made it and had a great time.

Just about the time spring arrived, I realized that I was pregnant again. All I could think was, "What? So soon?" I could hardly believe it. I didn't want to be pregnant and I wondered if I could stand up under the stress of another pregnancy and a third child. Once again I sat upon the dune behind the ranch house and thought of what lay ahead for me. The peaceful mountains brought a calm over me and I knew that I would endure.

I don't think I ever mustered the courage to tell Roy about this pregnancy. Somehow I just thought that if I ignored it, no one would pay much attention to it. In later years, I realized that Roy, having tested and doctored pregnant cows and birthed, pulled, and treated newborn calves, probably knew before I did when I was pregnant. I carried on as usual and the pregnancy never entered into our conversations in the beginning.

I spent most of my summer at the ranch and my pregnancy went as the others had. I had little trouble and continued with my daily chores. I really did not expect my baby until some time in late October or early November, so I had not made plans to move into town until the middle of October. On September 1 Roy and I did take a trip into town for supplies and a visit. While I was there I experienced some labor pains, even though I knew it was not time for my baby's birth. Roy sent for the doctor and shortly thereafter I had a new son, born on September 7, 1922.

We named this son Guy Crawford, after my father. Guy was a delicate baby, probably because of his being born at seven months. From his first days, he could not retain his food, and I spent day and night struggling to keep him alive. This process went on for months, and by the time he was eight months old he had not gained a single ounce in weight. He appeared to me to be all eyes. I devoted most of my time to Guy, continuing to nurse him the best I could and praying that he would survive. I had to depend on Rita to care for my other two children because Guy needed my constant care.

The doctor had told us that Guy had pyloric problems. He told us that surgery could be performed, but Roy and I chose not to have it done. Another infant from Marathon had had the same problem; his parents had taken him to San Antonio for surgery, but the child had died. We chose to feed Guy every hour in hopes that his body would retain enough food to keep him alive, because most of what he ate always came back up.

My hopes strengthened when he finally overcame his problem some eight months after his birth. He slowly began to retain food and gain weight. I had been rewarded by my constant care, and by the time he was two years old his eyes were not so prominent and he was a normal, beautiful baby.

By the time Guy was two, we had a house full of toddlers; Son was now four, and Dadie three. There were rare moments of peace, but most of the time was spent tending to children, household chores, and ranch duties.

Because most of our time was spent in town when Guy was a baby, I could depend on friends for comfort and companionship. Margaret

Buttrill was in my home regularly. I had begun to look upon her as a part of the family and depended on her for advice. Unfortunately, at one point she had to make a long trip to San Antonio and was gone for several weeks. When she returned she took one look at me and exclaimed, "Young lady, have you been on the scales lately? You are skin and bones. What in the world is happening to you? Are you sick?"

I assured Margaret that I was well. I knew that I had lost weight; in fact, I had gone from my usual one hundred fifty-six pounds to one hundred sixteen pounds. I suddenly realized that I looked terrible. Even Roy had complained about my weight. He said to me one day, "I thought I married a fat girl, and now look at you. I want you back good and fat. I like fat women."

I supposed that having three babies so soon after the siege of influenza had taken its toll. I really did look like something the cats dragged in. I knew that the only thing I needed was the ranch. I told Roy, "Let's get back to the ranch, I need my rock on the sand pile, I need my Maravillas Canyon, the mountains, and our cows and horses. I need to hear and see the geese fly over our land."

At that point, we closed up the town house, loaded the car with the children and Rita, and headed back home to the ranch. As we approached the ranch house I had the feeling that "my cup runneth over with joy." I was so excited as we approached the ranch that I began to think of my childhood days when we lived on a cattle ranch in the mountains between Sanderson and Fort Stockton. When I was four and five years old, my older brother Frank, my older sister Mabel, and I had stick horses to ride and cow horns for our cows. We even had a few corn cobs for our sheep. It was fun getting sotol stalks to make our stick horses and gathering up those old horns for cows. We would build play-pastures, using rock for fences. I hoped that our children would have as much imagination and enjoy the ranch life ahead of them as I did when I was a child.

As we reestablished our lives at the ranch, I began to watch my children grow and play. I never got to see them ride stick horses, since they were all placed upon a real horse at an early age. They were riding alone by the time they were three years old. I did enjoy watching them play in the sand pile, romp through the pastures and nearby creek beds, drive imaginary trucks, and ride their modern-day tricycles. They were normal children and enjoyed their childhood years.

I used to listen as my children played around the ranch. They had created their own little world and worked it as though there was noth-

13. Guy, Dadie, and Son at house in town, 1928

ing else around them. Guy, being the frail one, always followed after Son and Dadie. He depended on them most of the time, and they often did his chores for him. Guy used to tell me, whenever I asked him to get an egg from the henhouse or bring in a vegetable from the garden, "Mama, I too tired!" He used that expression repeatedly.

One day I was beside the barn and the children were playing inside it. I could hear them talking. Dadie spotted a bee and mentioned to the others, "Mama said she needed some honey but the bees won't make it for her." No one said anything for a moment and then Guy chirped out, "They too tired!"

Of course, the bees couldn't provide me with honey because we had had little rain and there were no blossoms. But I always enjoyed the children's point of view on life. I often wonder if most people ever get to experience the true unity of a family as I did. I know that city life is different and ranch life is hard, but with nothing else but my family around me, I feel that I have bonds with my children that few ever get an opportunity to experience, and I owe most of this to Roy and the ranch.

Son was large for his age. His baby days had been cut short since the other two babies came along so quickly. Roy was more than happy when Son was three years of age so he could put him on a horse and make a cowboy of him. One of Roy's greatest pleasures came when he bought Son's first pair of boots and spurs. Of course, a saddle came soon after these. I felt pride in my son when he mounted his horse and rode off with Roy to the mountains. I also felt an emptiness. I was experiencing Son "cutting the apron springs" and realizing that Son was becoming his father's child and not his mother's. I watched him grow up quickly and realized that he would never get to ride stick horses and play cowboys; he was becoming a real one.

Roy and Son rode off together one day and returned much later than I had expected. I asked, "What kept you so long?"

Roy laughingly told me this story. He said that they had been looking for two certain cows. They had found only one of them near the Black Hill tank. Roy told Son to watch that old cow while he went off to look for the other cow. After a while Roy returned with the second cow to the spot where he had left Son. There sat Son on his horse just where Roy had left him, but there was no cow in sight. Roy rode up to Son and said, "Son, I thought I told you to watch that cow until I got back."

Son replied, "I did, Daddy, as long as I could see her."

Roy and Son had to hunt the cow again and Roy realized that he should have told Son to keep the cow there instead of telling him to watch her. Son had done exactly as he had been told. Roy and I had a big laugh about it after the children had gone to bed. That experience made me think of the times when I thought I was doing exactly what Roy wanted, only to find out that I had done something completely different. It seems as though life with Roy was always exciting – somehow complex and simple at the same time.

I watched as my children adapted to and accepted their lives on the ranch. They always adjusted to any given situation on the ranch. They could work if need be, entertain themselves whenever necessary, and function as normal children. I remember thinking one day as I watched the three playing in the sand pile, "I hope our lives will always be this way."

Illness Strikes

My first child, Son, seemed to have been born almost grown. I depended on him to help around the house whenever I was ill, had to help Roy, or had other pressing matters to attend to. He grew up quickly. Dadie came so soon after Son, and Guy so soon after Dadie, that I was not able to pay much attention to Dadie. I had to spend much time with Guy as an infant, and Dadie was usually watched over by Son. One day Mrs. Buttrill came to the ranch and gasped, "Are you ever going to let that child out of her 'kiddie coop'?" Dadie would sit in her makeshift playpen for hours just watching the world go by and rubbing the hem of a diaper. She gave me little trouble, so many people thought that she lacked attention. Believe me, when I couldn't give my children attention, there were Roy, Rita, and the boys to fill in. We stayed one big happy family.

In the period of time when my babies were growing up into children, changes were occurring fast and furiously. There was never a dull moment. The children exerted tremendous energy all the time whether at work or play. Their playtimes were spent in the Maravillas Canyon exploring Indian caves and splashing in the water holes that were left after a big rain. But there was not much time for play, as Roy had them working and riding with him at early ages. He believed that their early training was important in what they would become later in their lives, and I never questioned him.

Roy and I would often be very tired and ready to relax in the shade of the arbor or stretch out on a bed, but the children would be playing cowboys and Indians or digging a would-be fortress on the dune. They just never seem to tire. They kept me constantly aware of their presence.

My sessions on the rock behind the kitchen grew further and further apart, but at times I was compelled to vanish from the chatter of the children and take to my rock. There I could gather my thoughts and have my dreams for the future as well as think of happy days of the past.

While we were at the ranch, I received the joyous news that Papa and Mama were ready to come back to Texas. They had spent enough time in Arizona. My brother Alvin had gone to California and soon afterwards married his first and only sweetheart, Doris Freeman. They were happy in California and settled there. By that time, my sister Lovenia had graduated from Phoenix High School and had taken a position in a bank there. My sister Mabel, her husband Henry, and their family were apparently settled in Phoenix, so Papa and Mama, with the last of their six children, Glen, were to move back to Texas. I could hardly wait for their arrival.

When they arrived in Texas, they decided to visit with us in Marathon. Roy and I, as were the children, were happy to have Papa and Mama with us. We stayed in town most of the time, but also went to the ranch for a visit. Roy showed Papa the ranch and the cattle. We would have loved having them live with us; however, Papa had another idea. He had been offered a position with the Combs Cattle Company and had accepted the job. He, Mama, and Glen moved to "The Gap," some twenty miles south of Marathon, and settled there for a year.

While at the ranch, Mama was horrified at seeing all our guns in the house. She exclaimed one day, "Daughter, are those guns loaded?"

"Yes, Mama. Every gun is loaded and there is a gun handy in every room," I explained.

"Do you mean to say that you keep loaded guns where the children can get then?" She asked.

"Yes, we have told the children to leave the guns alone. They have never touched one of them." I then explained to Mama what Roy had told me earlier. "When you need to use a gun, there isn't time to look for cartridges or load it. The gun should be already loaded or it'll be too late." I told Mama that we had always lived by that rule.

Mama and I did not always agree on how my children should be reared. Roy had to work cattle one day while Mama and Papa were visiting. She and I sat under the arbor and visited while the men gathered, marked, branded, wormed, and castrated our new calves. Son had been in the pen helping Roy until the castrating began. He then came running up to me with a shocked look on his face and fearfully asked, "Mama, why – why – why is Daddy making the baby calves bleed?"

I looked at Son and calmly spoke. "Son, those are all bull calves. Daddy does not want them all to be bulls. Too many bulls will cause problems in a herd. He will take a small part of their body out and they will not cause problems for the rest of the herd and we can sell them for more money at market." Son quickly accepted my answer and ran back over to the pens.

I turned to Mama, who was as white as a ghost. She gasped, "Daughter, that is not your job to answer such questions. That's Roy's job! You shouldn't discuss such things with your son!" Then she exclaimed. "Daughter, don't say that word *bull,* either."

"What should I say?" I asked.

"Well, you can say *cow.*"

I promptly explained to Mama, "A cow is not a bull!"

"Well, call it a steer. Just don't say that word and don't answer any more of Son's questions. Let Roy do it."

I simply answered Mama, "Son didn't ask Roy, he asked me!"

I thought of Mama and her pure southern upbringing. There were just certain things one did not mention in the presence of ladies, and I often found Mama shocked at some of the things we discussed about the ranch. After that conversation, I tried to be more careful about what I said around Mama. She was aghast at any discussion of calf pulling, castrating, or worming, and she disapproved of any "foul" language of any sort. Roy and I both worked to "hold our tongues" whenever Mama was around, and she felt much better when she thought all was kept "respectful for a lady," something she continually tried to make me be.

It was comforting to me to have my parents nearby. They were very understanding and helpful when I needed them, so I worked to make them comfortable and welcome.

After Mama and Papa settled at "The Gap," I had been so busy and involved with our daily routine of ranch work, caring for home duties and children's needs, that I had not recognized a change in Roy. I noticed that one day he sat down to rest after having walked a very short distance. He got up after a short time and came into the house. I noticed immediately that he was very pale and out of breath.

"What's wrong with you? Come, lie down on the bed," I urged.

"I don't know. I'll be all right after I rest a while," he replied.

Several days went by and Roy did not improve. I was really worried about him. When I saw that he was failing in health every day, I decided to take him to a doctor. In Marathon, Dr. Worthington said for me to take him to San Antonio immediately. I called my friends in San Antonio, Louie and Margaret Hess, and asked them to meet us at the depot there. I just told them that Roy was sick and we were arriving on the train.

The train arrived in the city at three o'clock in the morning. Louie and Margaret were there to meet us and took us straight to Dr. Milburn's clinic. The doctor was there expecting us and in a short time Roy was being examined.

The Hesses – Louie, Margaret, and Uncle Charlie – were some of Roy's lifelong friends. They had come from Ohio to Marathon in the 1880s and established a large ranch some ten miles north of Marathon. They also owned and operated a general merchandise store in Marathon. Roy had considered the Hess family as some of his best friends. The Hess Mercantile was the place for cowmen to trade and do their banking, and most men would look for Louie Hess when they were in trouble and needed help.

As I waited for Roy's examination to be complete, I thought over the times when Roy had depended on Louie Hess. Once when Roy was called to federal jury duty in El Paso, he went to Hess and told him that he needed fifty dollars for the trip. Mr. Hess, being a very conservative man, asked if he could not make the trip on twenty-five dollars. Roy accepted the money and left for El Paso.

While in El Paso, Roy and some of his friends decided to visit Juarez. Of course, they got involved in a poker game. Roy ended up losing big in that game and he had to get a draft of three hundred dollars on Mr. Hess to cover his debts.

Upon Roy's return to Marathon, he first went to Louie and told him, "Louie, I had to draw a three-hundred-dollar draft on you in Juarez."

Louie Hess stared at Roy speechless for a moment and then asked, "Roy, can you do that?"

"Well, I did!"

Mr. Hess accepted the response and just shook his head. He always knew that Roy was good for his word.

It was "true to form" that we called on the Hesses when Roy became ill. They took me into their home while Roy was in the clinic. After the tests were completed, Dr. Milburn said that we could go home. Dr. Milburn explained to me that Roy was in the final stages of tuberculosis. He said, "With good care, Roy might live for six weeks." He told me to keep him comfortable and said that that would be all that I could do. With this information, we boarded the train and headed home.

Word was soon spread in Marathon that Roy was a dying man. Friends and neighbors came offering help and advice. I knew then that the best people in the world lived in Marathon and the Big Bend area. Even Roy's friends in Mexico heard of his illness and sent medicine for him, including herbs of various kinds that were sure to make him well, or so they thought. I fed and doctored Roy the best I could. I fixed a bed on the front porch for him so he would feel out in the open and not hemmed in.

Some of Roy's friends from Alpine, Angie and Jim Wilson, Joe Hord, and Dr. Craddock, came to visit Roy. That particular day was one of Roy's worst. Dr. Craddock examined Roy carefully, took his blood pressure, and checked his pulse. We then walked inside the house and he told me that Roy would probably not make it through the night. Angie and Jim asked me if I wanted them to stay with me, but I just shook my head, knowing that Roy would never want anyone there. He was just too proud. I thanked them for all they had done and sent them back home. That night I sat by Roy's side and watched every labored breath he took, wondering if it was his last. At one point, a time when I think even Roy thought that he was dying, he raised his head slightly from his pillow and looked straight into my eyes and said, "Take care of the children." I just prayed and nodded. Somehow Roy made it through that night, only to have to suffer many more. There were good days, though. Mrs. Ed Decie and Zetha Hicks, two of Roy's favorite people, came by to visit on one of his really bad days. They had him laughing and responding to their chatter in no time. I will always believe that they helped him to make it through another rough night.

Many things fell upon my shoulders while Roy was ill. Things that young women are never called upon to do were placed before me. While Roy was confined to his bed in Marathon, Uncle Bob and Baltazar, a Mexican Indian from the interior of Mexico who had shown up one day looking for work, were left to care for the ranch since Lee was at Dove Mountain. One hot afternoon, Baltazar and Uncle Bob ate a watermelon while they rested under the arbor. By sundown, Baltazar left to bring in the milch cow. When he returned, Uncle Bob was nowhere to be found. Baltazar searched everywhere for him, but as dark came he gave up his search until the next morning. He rose early and looked around the house once again for Uncle Bob. He found his body some hundred yards from the house on the sand pile. Baltazar said that he knew where the body was because he noticed the ranch dog standing guard over something on the sand pile. We all knew that the dog must have guarded the body all night long knowing that if he had not the coyotes or wolves would have dragged it off or fed upon it. Uncle Bob had apparently gotten sick from eating too much watermelon and died of a heart attack.

Word was brought to me about Uncle Bob. I had to send the law officials to investigate the death. They reported that Uncle Bob had evidently staggered toward the sand pile in pain, regurgitated some of the melon along the way, and fallen where he died.

I had to arrange for the funeral service and burial. I telephoned Uncle Bob's brother in Van Horn, and he told me to take care of everything. He said that he was too old to help and was unable even to attend the funeral. I had every detail to take care of alone. I did not bother Roy with any of the details, as I knew he was too ill and would worry about all the arrangements. I managed to get through that ordeal knowing that Uncle Bob had been my good friend and that I would lay him to rest the best that I knew how. I did what I had to do.

After a month's time of being in bed on the porch in Marathon, Roy said to me, "Bring me my pants, we're going to the ranch. I'll die if I stay in this bed."

I did not argue. We packed up and returned to the ranch. At the ranch, Roy rested for a few days and then told me to have Baltazar saddle his horse.

I protested, "You're not able to ride."

I just watched as Roy mounted his horse and rode off alone. He was gone about ten minutes before returning. He was out of breath and very weak. I put him back in the bed and watched him fight for life all through the night, barely able to breathe. I didn't know whether Roy would live another day. I often wondered what I would do if I lost him. I gathered my courage, held on, and tried to hope for the best.

The next morning, Roy was still alive and once again told Baltazar to saddle up his horse. That time he rode a little longer than the day before. I worried that he might not ride back home, but he did. He was exhausted. Again, I stood by watching him fight for life, not knowing which minute would be his last. The experience was horrifying.

This procedure of horseback riding continued with each day. And each day, his ride was a little longer than the one before. At night, I would lie awake wondering what to do. One thing that I did do was keep the children quiet so Roy could rest. I also fixed nourishing meals and hoped and prayed for his recovery. I guess that many things helped Roy recover and no one thing can be specifically held responsible unless it was Roy's determination to get on his horse and ride in the sunshine every day.

It was three months before Roy was able to saddle his own horse, but the day finally came. I watched as Roy struggled with the saddling of his horse, refusing any help. Not long after this, Son and I joined him often on his daily rides and before we knew it, we were all back into the routine of taking care of the necessary cow work. With the help of Baltazar to do the heavy work and Rita to care for Dadie and Guy, we once again settled down into our regular daily routine around the ranch.

It was not until Roy's recovery that I completely understood what courage, willpower, faith, and determination were. I look back and know that all of these characteristics were extremely important. Not only Roy had to sustain the hardships – our whole family did.

Baltazar

WITH Roy just regaining his health, he had to depend on the men around the ranch to do his work. Baltazar had shown up one day looking for work and Roy, being the kind and generous man he was, hired him, knowing that the old man knew little about ranching. Still, Baltazar tried hard and proved to Roy that he was a good worker and could be depended upon. Baltazar was a real blessing around the place after Uncle Bob passed away.

Roy took Baltazar with him on a ride into the mountains one day. I think Roy wanted to go just "to see what he could see." It was a way for Roy to ride in the sunshine and regain his strength.

The two men ended up in the Stillwell Mountains, where a small canyon was formed. Often the Stillwell cattle were located in that area, where they were sometimes difficult to find. As the two men got off their horses and looked around, Roy wished aloud, "If I had the money and knowhow, I'd dam up this canyon and give our cattle up here a good watering hole. It could also be a holding tank for water during the dry spells." With that he started to mount his horse.

Baltazar stopped him and told him in Spanish, "I can build that dam for you. I know how."

Roy just scoffed and grunted at the old man, "Why, we don't have the necessary materials or the money to buy them!"

The old man looked Roy right in the eye and said quite assuredly, "I can make the materials and build the dam. I know how. I don't know much about ranching and cattle, but I can build anything. You just tell me and I'll have it built for you."

Roy looked at the old man and nodded. He felt that nothing would be harmed if the old man couldn't build the dam, and if he could, the ranch would certainly be much better. Baltazar would have plenty to do for awhile. Roy came home that night and told me this story, and I knew that he wasn't so sure Baltazar could make the materials needed for a holding tank.

The next day Baltazar was up early. He went down to the Maravillas Creek and dug around all morning long. I found out that he had dug a hole about six feet wide and fifteen feet deep. Next he walked through the pastures and searched for wood. He hitched up an old wagon of ours to two mules and spent that afternoon searching for and collecting wood. He then returned to his hole in the Maravillas, which he filled with wood. He then started the wood to burning. This burning process went on for a solid week.

Once the hole was half full of wood ashes, he collected creek rocks from the Maravillas Creek bed. Once again he put the wagon and mules to work. He carted those rocks down the creek and placed every one, specially chosen, on top of the wood ashes in the hole.

Again, Baltazar started hauling wood to the hole. This time, he placed the wood on top of the rocks and started another bonfire. This burning process took several days. Once that batch of wood had burned, he finished filling up the hole with sand from the creek. On top of all of this matter, Baltazar placed more wood. This he burned for several more days.

I watched curiously for a complete month as Baltazar worked diligently down in the creek. I asked Roy one day how the old man was doing and he quickly told me, "I don't have time to check on him. He's doing fine." I wondered if we'd ever see a finished project, but like Roy I believed that any man who went to that much trouble would surely produce.

After a month, Baltazar opened up his hole and began to shovel out the debris. Once he got to the layer of creek rocks, he had a beautiful layer of live lime. He gently shoveled this substance into the wagon and headed for the house.

As he drove into the yard, Roy met him. They both walked around to the wagon bed and Baltazar proudly displayed his beautiful white and perfectly powdered live lime.

Roy yelled at me from the wagon, "Hallie, get out here and see what we've got!"

I picked myself up and headed toward the wagon. I knew that Roy was excited about something. When I got there, Roy proudly showed me the perfect lime. He poured a little out on the ground. He walked to the trough, got a cup of water, and brought it over and poured it on the lime that was lying on the ground. Once the beads of water hit the lime, it began to hiss and steam. I knew then what Roy meant when he kept talking about "live lime." I asked Roy why he was so proud of this lime and he told me, "I'd have to spend a fortune buying and hauling materials into the mountains to build such a dam. That live lime mixed correctly with the right amounts of sand and water will make a perfect mortar and is better than concrete. It will hold those rocks together for centuries."

Within several weeks, Baltazar had the dam complete. Roy was so proud of that "rock header." He told everyone about his new addition to the ranch. When the first rains came, Roy and Baltazar rode up to the header to check it out. There in front of them was a perfect holding tank filled to the brim. Roy came home whistling that day.

Every time a good rain came, Roy would saddle up and check the water holes. Always the one that would be in the best shape was the one that Baltazar built. That old man was big and strong and had certainly learned much from his Indian tribe in Mexico. We were very thankful for his gift, the "live lime."

To this very day, that rock header is as effective as it was the day it was built by old Baltazar. It has provided many a Stillwell cow with much-needed water in rough times. Although Baltazar wasn't a ranch hand, he certainly left behind contributions to the ranch that have lasted several lifetimes.

The Bittersweet

I always felt that I was riding a roller coaster when I was married to Roy; it was great fun but I never knew what to expect around the next bend. There were times when Roy would be so proud of me that he could "cattle call" my success to the world. And then there were times when I wanted to dig a deep hole and pull the top in after me. I remember one time Roy told me, "Pat you on the back and you end up breaking your fool neck!" Needless to say, I received few praises from my husband. He never really scolded me either, but I always knew when I had done something wrong.

I learned to read Roy like Indian signs, subtle but clear. I knew when Roy was "riding loose." There would be hell to pay when he got off his horse. I figured out that I could watch the position of Roy on his horse, how he rode his horse, and how he carried himself when he rode or walked. Each of these positions meant something to me. Roy could read weather signs and animal tracks better than most Indians, but I could read human signs, his in particular, better than most. I had to in order to survive on the ranch. Of course, some I read were clearer to me than others.

I remember when I first noticed these signs. We were riding under the bluff and looking for a lost cow and her yearling calf. Roy knew that that cow was around that area because he had studied her tracks closely. There we were looking for a lost cow and her calf in among the most beautiful wildflowers I had ever seen in my life. I really wasn't too interested in those two animals, but I knew that I had to have a bouquet of those flowers for our dinner table that night. I glanced around, saw no cow or calf, and realized that Roy was paying me little attention. I just couldn't pass up the opportunity.

I slithered off my horse and just walked among the flowers for a moment. I looked around again and then gathered a huge bunch of those gorgeous wildflowers. I got back up on my horse and carried the bouquet on my arm. I was truly excited about finding such color-ful beauty in such sandy-colored terrain. I rode toward Roy and when I was about two hundred yards from him I noticed that he was still studying the tracks. I caught up to him and he gave me a fleeting glance, but not a word was said.

I followed close to him and we soon found the cow and calf. We tried to herd them toward home but they really gave us some trouble. The cow was jumpy and nervous. Roy wasn't able to keep the two contained. They ran in all directions and he was becoming quite frus-trated with the animals. I knew that Roy needed help, so I took my flowers and placed them safely under a dagger bloom in the shade and then rode over to help. I fully intended to return for my bouquet.

All the way home, we fought that cow and her yearling. When we finally made it home, the yearling refused to enter the pasture through the gate. Roy ended up having to rope the calf and drag it into the pas-ture. He gave me one swift look and took off on his horse. I watched as he rode off and noticed how loosely he was riding. I thought to myself, "Uh-oh, he's riding loose!"

When we got to the house, Roy was tired, sweaty, and angry for some reason. He hurriedly unsaddled his horse and stormed into the house. I turned my horse back to the mountains and my bouquet. I had no idea what was wrong with my husband.

I returned with my table arrangement. I prepared a nice meal and placed the flowers in the center of the table, and then stood back and thought how lovely they were. I hoped that the men would notice and say something about them.

Jona asked Roy about his day about midway through the meal. "I fought that old cow and her yearling all the way home," he said. "I didn't think I'd ever get them here!"

Lee knew that Roy was exhausted so he quickly changed the sub-ject. "Hallie, where did you get those flowers?"

"I found them under the bluff."

Roy interjected, "Yeah, it was that damn bunch of red flowers that startled that old cow in the first place. Hell, our cows don't know what to expect when a big red bunch of flowers comes after them!"

I knew once again I had "flubbed the dub." We all finished that meal in silence.

Roy never apologized, but he did get over his mad spells pretty quickly. The day after the flower incident, he had to take a long ride to look for some cattle that he knew were some eight or ten miles from home, and he said that I should stay home since it would be in rough country and under the bluff. As Roy rode off, I decided to spend my day arrowhead hunting and exploring Indian shelters. I thought that it would be a good way to pass the day and forget about his anger.

I was home early and when Roy came in that evening he seemed in better spirits. He wasn't in the house long when he asked, "Would you like to kill a mountain lion?"

"Yes, I sure would!" I answered in excitement.

Roy then began to explain his question in a serious matter. "I found the tracks of a big lion and saw where he had killed a deer. He covered the carcass up after he had eaten all he wanted of it for awhile. Since he covered the remains, he'll return to eat again. You can find him there in the morning."

Early the next morning, I saddled my horse, loaded my .30 .30 rifle, and set out in search of that mountain lion with great anticipation. Roy had described the vicinity where the lion had left the deer, and I did not have to look very long before I found the covered remains and the lion feeding. I got in good shooting distance of the lion and he never moved. He just kept eating. I eased from my saddle and carefully pulled my rifle from the saddle holster. I knew that I had to kill him with my first shot, or he might come at me. I was very nervous; my heart was pounding, and my knees were shaking something awful as I took careful aim.

I readied myself with gun to my shoulder. The lion sensed my presence and turned to face me. I aimed but did not budge. I got his head in my sights, held my breath, and squeezed the trigger. The blast rang in my ears as I watched the lion drop. The bullet had penetrated right between his eyes. I shook for a moment and almost dropped to the ground just from the fright and excitement. Just after the lion dropped, my horse jumped and ran. Furthermore, I could hardly eject the empty shell from the bullet chamber. I was shaking but I held together. I had to find my horse. I started after him and caught up to him some three hundred yards from the carcass. I knew that he was as frightened as I was. With trembling arms and shaking hands, I got on my horse and returned to get my gun. I placed the gun back in its scabbard, gathered the horse's reins, mounted, and started for home in a high lope.

As I rode into the house trap, Roy was waiting for me. He knew I was all right and didn't ask questions. He waited for me to tell my story. I could see in his face that he was proud of me. I felt proud of myself, too. I did not disclose to him my fear or the weakness that I had shown during the hunt and kill. I did not confess about my trem-

14. Hallie and Roy with Hallie's mountain lion

bling knees and shaking limbs. I did not tell him how I could hardly clear the empty shell from the gun chamber. I did enjoy expounding upon my victory.

Together, Roy and I took to the site of the kill a packhorse on which we would load the mountain lion to bring it home. We had little trouble achieving this as the packhorse was used to this type of carrying. We brought the lion home and immediately began to skin him. Roy estimated that he weighed over one hundred and fifty pounds. We measured him at six feet from tip of tail to tip of nose.

Roy told me I could have his hide made into a rug, which I did. I used it in the living room of our house in Marathon and it soon became a conversation piece.

I kept the rug for years, and it was always a remembrance of one of the times that I pleased Roy so. Even though I had many times disappointed Roy, the times he praised me or showed me acceptance

104

made up for his anger. I knew that life would always be bittersweet as long as I was married to him.

Life Continues

As my children grew I watched the ranch prosper and Roy work harder and harder even though he was not completely well. I still worked with the men but also had to spend time tending to the children, as I no longer had Rita. She had married and started a home of her own. Son was a great deal of help as he had turned nine years old and was quite large for his age. He often worked as hard as the men. Dadie, at seven years old, had taken over many of the household chores when she was not riding with us, and Guy, who was five, was always astride a horse. He wasn't much help on the ground but he could manage a horse well enough to be help when working stock. As 1928 rolled around I felt that things were improving.

Summer was once again upon us and the heat was stifling. I spent most of my time enjoying the arbor while I watched my children romp and play in the sand pile or haystack. The heat never seemed to bother them much. As I was enjoying the coolness of the arbor one day, I heard Dadie crying. I jumped up and saw her riding her tricycle as fast as she could toward the house. Dadie was using one arm to guide her trike and the other was hanging limply by her side. I got to her as fast as I could and knew her arm was hurt.

I called to Roy. "Roy, come quickly! Dadie's hurt!"

Roy hurried to the arbor, took one look at Dadie's arm, and realized her arm was broken.

Between her sobs she told me she had fallen from the haystack. I wasn't sure what to do. I just looked at Roy.

"We'll have to take her to Alpine. Let Dr. Craddock take a look at it. Dr. Worthington in Marathon can't set broken bones."

I bustled around haphazardly and managed to get things ready for a trip to Alpine. Roy gathered up Guy and Son and in minutes we were on our way. I fixed up a pillow for Dadie's arm so the rough ride on the rocky road wouldn't hurt her.

We arrived in Alpine around midnight. Dadie had hurt all the way to town. We immediately went to Dr. Craddock's house and awakened him. He sent us to his office downtown, where he met us shortly. I gathered up Dadie in my arms and hurried into the office. I just left

Guy and Son sleeping in the car. Dr. Craddock placed Dadie on his examination table and said to Roy, "Roy, you'll have to hold her down while I check her arm."

Roy held tightly to Dadie while Dr. Craddock looked closely at her arm. I guess he knew that he had better set the arm immediately. With Dadie screaming and fighting and Roy holding her securely, Dr. Craddock snapped the arm back into place. I limply crumpled to the floor.

When I "came to," Dadie was sitting on the table with her arm neatly bandaged and splinted. I missed most of the repair work on my daughter's arm because I had fainted. The men had just left me on the floor and continued on with Dadie. I guess I was less trouble to them in that condition.

Dr. Craddock explained that there was no x-ray machine in Alpine. He wanted us to go to Marfa the next day and get Dadie's arm x-rayed to make sure it was set properly. We went to the Holland Hotel, got a room, and slept for a few hours. The next morning we took Dadie to the doctor in Marfa, where we found out that her arm was securely set. From there we headed back to Marathon. From this incident I learned that a ranchwoman must not only have courage and tenacity, but composure, something I had lost in the doctor's office. I never got much better at it either. I could kill an animal, cut a calf, defend myself at any time, but when it came to my children and their pains, I was pretty useless.

We stayed in Marathon for several days while Dadie got used to her bandaged arm. We wanted to make sure that we wouldn't have to make another fast trip to Alpine. At the end of the week, we took Dadie to Alpine for a checkup. The doctor was surprised as he examined her. "This beats anything I've ever seen. Her arm is healing perfectly. You're lucky!" With such a good report, we returned to the ranch.

I had a Mexican woman to stay with Dadie while I rode with Roy. We worked the cattle with the help of some good cowboys. September came and Son was of school age. I knew that I had to stay at the ranch and ride every day with Roy. I had only one choice. I decided to send Son to my sister Mabel who lived in Phoenix, Arizona. She could see that he would attend school. That was one of the hardest things I ever had to do. My firstborn was only five years old and I was sending him away for nine months. My consolation was that he would be in good hands and with someone who would care for and love him just as I would.

When Son came home in the summer for vacation I realized how

15. Roy, Hallie, and Thomas Mitchell (cousin) at house in town, 1925

terribly I had missed him. When he arrived at the ranch, he just looked around for a few minutes and then ran around to the back of the house. I ran after him and found him standing alone just crying. I asked him what troubled him.

He sniffled a reply. "It's been so long. I didn't know I had been gone so long." I never sent Son back. He would stay home. I made up my mind at that moment that my children would go to school in Marathon. Roy and I would just have to adjust.

After Roy's first sickness in 1925, Roy suffered pain off and on for three years. During the summer months Son, Dadie, Guy, and I would help Roy and the men every day, but when school started I had to move to town. I really hated leaving Roy alone knowing that he was not in good health, but I had to consider our children's education. Once again I had to make a decision that was extremely difficult.

In the fall of 1928, Roy suffered a severe attack of appendicitis. Off we went again by train to Dr. Milburn in San Antonio. I knew of no other place to take Roy. Again Louie and Margaret Hess met the train at three o'clock in the morning. They rushed us to the clinic.

After a short examination, Dr. Milburn told me that he did not know if Roy would make it. He felt that Roy's only chance was an operation, a chance he felt he had to take. To Dr. Milburn's surprise, Roy made it through the surgery. Dr. Milburn had removed his appendix.

Dr. Milburn never indicated that Roy's problem over the past few years had been his appendix, but I felt that a bad appendix over a period of years weakened Roy's body to the point that he had no resistance to the tubercular germ. Because of the lack of good medical care on the ranch, we often had to deal with our own problems. Dr. Milburn had only seen Roy once before and neither Roy nor I ever blamed him for a bad diagnosis. I just felt that Dr. Milburn was not aware of the intense pain Roy had suffered in the past and he did the best that he could with the knowledge that he had.

Dr. Milburn did give Roy some pretty stern advice. "Roy, you are not going to be able to work. You need to sit on the fence and let someone else just do the work. Take it easy and enjoy life."

Roy adamantly replied, "When I can't do my own work, I want to be dead!" Dr. Milburn just shook his head and let us leave. I think he knew what Roy would do. I thought back to the time when Dr. Milburn told Roy earlier that moving to a better climate would improve his health. Once again Roy showed his love for the ranch and the West Texas area with his curt reply, "I'd rather be dead in Marathon than alive somewhere else." As we left Dr. Milburn's office, the man was still shaking his head.

Once out of the doctor's office, Roy said that we certainly didn't have any more business in San Antonio and we packed our things, boarded the next train, and went to Marathon. Being home always seemed to make Roy feel better and we both were relieved to have Roy's problem solved.

After a few weeks of recovery, we were able to return on weekends and holidays to the ranch, where Roy's health improved greatly. I can remember those days of recuperating. Roy sat in the saddle and roped calves all day, but he was not able to do one thing on the ground. Son and I did the ground work. Roy roped a calf by its two hind hooves, and I threw the calf down and Son tied its legs together. Sometimes Son and I exchanged jobs. We managed to mark and brand all our calves this way. I soon realized that there was always work to be done on the ranch even if we did have good Mexican help. There were some things that Roy felt only Son or I could do. He did love having his family as a working team. Guy usually stayed in his saddle as we worked and Dadie took over the house. Once again our team was in full force.

I watched as Roy gained more and more strength. It was amazing to me that a man who had been ill for so long and so near death could recover as Roy did. While he never did get to be what one would call a completely "well man," he was able to lead a fairly active life. The doctor had told Roy that he could never work again but we all knew that Roy would prove him wrong or die trying.

With such determination, Roy slowly recovered and did most of his own work. Roy remained the man in charge and the man who did the work for the remaining years of his life. He stayed a man who would not shirk his duty as a good citizen, father, or ranch hand. He was always willing to help anyone who needed him and he kept his winning smile. His friends remained in awe of his courage and determination. I was thankful.

Drought

Dry weather had been creeping up on the country for several months; however, we ranch people took it as a usual matter. I did notice, though, that Roy was getting more and more concerned, indulging in more "silent spells" and tossing in bed at night. He seemed to have an inner feeling of disaster, but he tried to shield me from his worries.

Most of my time was now spent in town as the children were in school. I knew that Roy was concerned, but I thought his concerns were just minor ranch problems. Little did I know that Roy's intuition was certainly indicative of what was ahead of us.

Our children were happy in school and I kept more than busy with everyday chores. In the early spring of 1930, as I attended the interscholastic meet being held in the Marathon school, in which my three children participated, my attention was suddenly attracted to the mountains and in a northward direction. I saw a huge dark cloud of brownish red rolling over the tops of the mountains, and it appeared to be crawling, covering the entire world as it crept toward us.

"Look!" I shouted at the school superintendent. "What's that creeping over the mountains?"

He replied, "It looks like a cloud and it's coming this way."

I did not like the looks of that cloud. I had never seen anything like that crawling blanket. I felt that we would soon be covered. I asked permission to take my children out of the contests, gathered them up, loaded my car, locked up the house, and headed for the security of Roy and the ranch. I hoped to outrun the rolling cloud, which I soon realized was a dust cloud, but it overtook me just as I arrived at the ranch house. I was relieved of my panic when Roy helped us into the house and closed all the doors and windows to protect us from that red-brown dust rolling over the countryside. We might as well have left the house wide open, though – nothing, absolutely nothing, kept that dust out of our house. Darkness was upon us even though the sun was still high in the sky. The chickens went to roost, the milch cow bawled for her calf, and the saddle horses came early for their feed. The scenario was strange and unknown to me.

Roy said that we could not risk building a fire in the wood cook-stove to cook supper for fear that the wind would catch a spark and set the dry parched area on fire. We could not go outside, so it would be impossible to do the evening chores. All we could do at this point would be to just go to bed and cover our heads, and that we did. The wind howled all that day but finally died down in the night. When I awoke the next morning, I noticed that I could see where my head had been on the pillow, as dust had settled all over our bed and everything else in the house. Outside the dust storm had left its "calling card." Skies were gray and our dear mountains were dim and looked far away. This was our first experience of the many dust storms that plagued our nation that year. Our country was already in a state of depression. The stock market crash of 1929 and the closing of many banks and money-lending institutions had devastated the country. It was a time when many suffered.

Farmers in Kansas and other farm states were not prepared for this big change in weather conditions, commonly known as a drought. These farmers began to watch their beautiful farms turn into "dust bowls" and their rich topsoil ride the high dry winds to goodness knows where. Much of their soil blew into Texas in the form of those red-brown dust clouds. The Big Bend area and our ranch received their share of the dust, and our ranchmen began to realize that the American economy, and therefore also the West Texas economy, had finally hit bottom.

President Roosevelt, newly elected to office, soon started the government wheels working to get relief to those in need. People out of work were riding freight trains or walking the highways through the country looking and hoping for help. A government agency, called the Regional Agriculture Credit Corporation (RACC), was set up to organize help for ranchmen and farmers in West Texas. An office was set up in San Angelo to serve our region. As the Marathon State Bank closed and the merchants refused credit to ranchmen, Roy and I turned to the RACC. There we secured a loan. This loan was doled out to pay our outstanding debts and to provide for fuel, ranch expenses, and taxes. We were allowed fifty dollars per month for our family of five for living expenses. As I sized up the ten dollars a month that each of us would be allotted, I knew that the living would be slim and a lot of belt-tightening would have to take place. I could plainly see the writing on the wall.

"We can't send the children to school," I said to Roy shortly after my realization of our family's economic status. I knew we would have to make sacrifices.

But Roy quickly replied, "The children will go to school regardless. We'll manage somehow." This was really what I had wanted to hear. I realized that Roy was as willing as I to make every sacrifice possible to educate our children.

As the months passed, times got harder. There was still no rain, and the wind and clouds of dust continued to whip our land. Thousands of cattle, sheep, and goats, and much wildlife, perished for want of food and water. Our ranch neighbors were as badly off as we were, and some of them gave up and left. Roy and I felt that we had too much at stake to leave, and we did not want to lose our land. It was the ranchmen who were leasing land that were the ones hardest hit by the drought, and it was these men who threw in the towel first.

Government inspectors for the RACC loan came quite often to check our herd of cattle and make reports to the government on our situation. On our first inspection, I was caught unaware and suffered much embarrassment.

Roy had told me to go before sunup and bring in a newborn calf and its mother that were in a pasture about two miles from the house. I saddled my horse early and rode away, leaving beds unmade and dishes unwashed, knowing that I had to get to the cow and calf before the sun rose and the heat intensified. As I was returning with the baby calf perched in the saddle with me, I saw that I had company at the house. As I rode up to the gate two strange men approached me and told me to hand them the calf, which I did. They then introduced themselves as Edwards and Oliver from Midland, inspectors for the RACC.

"Oh, my goodness!" I responded; I knew how awful I looked so early in the morning. I had not combed my hair or even put on a clean shirt.

"Where's Roy?" one of the men asked.

I was quick to reply. "He's gone to Dove Mountain and won't be back before late this evening." I hoped that the men would leave then, but instead they made themselves comfortable under the arbor as I tried to hide my embarrassment. The coffee was still warm on the stove and I added another stick of wood to the fire, and we soon had hot coffee. After giving them the coffee, I once again expected them to leave. They did not. While they sat there I told them, the best way I could, how we were getting along. I mentioned the two sotol camps we had going to help feed the cattle. I described how we divided the work, Roy going in one direction and I in another. I explained that if I found a cow down or stuck in a muddy tank, I would inform Roy and together we would pull it out. Finally, after all this talking and explaining, I noticed that dinner time was approaching.

I excused myself and went into the kitchen to fix a bite to eat (beans and bread). Of course I invited them to dinner, explaining that I had little to offer. They accepted. After we ate Oliver said, "I'll wash the dishes." I objected, but he insisted.

As I attempted to take over the dishwashing, Edwards exclaimed, "Let him wash 'em, he's good at dishwashing."

Oliver was already fixing dishwater and I began explaining how I had left so early for the baby calf. I apologized for leaving the break-fast dishes undone. Oliver looked around for a minute and promptly replied, "I don't think you washed your supper dishes either." I could have crawled under the table, but I made no explanation or apology.

Roy rode in on time, and I was more than glad to see him. He could talk to the two men while I went on with the delayed housework. Roy was glad to take over and liked both of the men – enough that he even invited them to spend the night. He told the men that in the morning he and I would go with them to inspect other ranches whose owners had loans with the RACC.

We were soon bedded down and were up quickly the next morn-ing. On the trip to surrounding ranches, Roy and I became better ac-quainted with the inspectors and they with us. All throughout the drought, Roy and I traveled with these inspectors and we all became very good friends.

Those trips were beneficial to Roy and me as we became better acquainted with neighbors and saw firsthand how they managed their ranch operations in those frightful times. We soon realized that all of us were in the same boat.

Now that our three children were all good help with ranch work, we as a family worked together to save the cattle and ranch. Kenneth Oliver said to me after observing our ranch operation one day, "Some-day you will realize that these hard days are the happiest days of your life. Your family is together and you're all working to save your land and cattle."

Each day brought a different challenge as we scanned the skies for hopes of rain, rain that would not come. Our cows became poor and weak and could not take care of their baby calves. Even though we lifted many of the cows to their feet when they were too weak to get up and tried to teach them to eat, they would often just give up and die.

Before Roy realized that we were in a drought, he had bought some steer yearlings from Gene Benson in Alpine for twenty-five dollars a head and brought them to the ranch. He had planned on keeping them for a year and then selling them at a nice price.

At the end of the year, the steers had grown and fattened, so Roy decided to sell them. He went to town and looked for a buyer. After talking to several buyers he had an offer of seven cents per pound. Roy refused that price and said that he would hold his steers for a better price.

When Roy told Lou Buttrill that he had refused the seven cents, Lou replied, "Roy, I think you'll see the day that you would be glad to get a nickel a pound."

We held on to the steers for another two years hoping for rain, hoping for better prices. Finally, when we could not feed or water those steers any longer we shipped them to Flint Hills in Kansas at a big expense for freight, pasturage, and care. We also had to sell the remainder of stock on our own ranch before winter came. We sold them for eighteen dollars a head. We had lived to see Lou Buttrill's prediction; we would have been better off selling our herd at a nickel a pound. We knew that there was no way to save our herd. Water was drying up and we had no grass. A drive of the herd to ship them someplace was an impossibility since there was no water or grass for them on the way to market.

The government came up with the plan of killing the cattle. They would pay twelve dollars per head for grown cattle and six dollars for calves. As a last resort and with tears in our eyes, we gathered the cows that were too weak to live and accepted the government offer; we shot our cattle. We herded them up against a bluff in the Maravillas Creek and let the government men mow them down with thirty-thirty rifles. They called it a mercy killing.

Our family could not eat supper that night following the shooting. I went to my rock on the sand pile, and Roy joined me on my rock for his first and only time. We sat in silence as we watched the sun go down in a red glaze. Roy finally remarked, "See that red sunset? That means another wind and dust storm tomorrow. We'll have to work hard to save the few cows we have left."

16. Big Bend ranchmen; Roy is near the center on a white horse

I knew what tomorrow would bring, and there were many more such days as the red sunsets continued. Our neighbor, Joe Graham, who ranched in the Rosillas Mountains, had brought in sheep to stock his ranch. Graham was a well-known, prominent West Texas ranchman. He had put together a large spread just before the drought set in. His sheep had been doing well in his good ranch country. However, the hot dry days and months that followed without rain soon had his sheep scattering out for food and water. Some of his flock ranged over our way and settled in the Stillwell Mountains. Here they became wild and fattened on desert shrubs in the high rocky cliffs. The only way one could get one was to use a thirty-thirty rifle. Roy told Joe Graham about his sheep being on our mountain and Joe said, "Roy, do whatever you can with them. I have sheep scattered all over the country. There's no way for me to save them."

Roy replied, "They're fat and will make good eating."

Joe quickly responded, "Then they're yours to eat."

Roy wasted no time in killing one and cooking it in a hole in the ground. We feasted for several days. In the following months we ate most of those sheep. Then I sheared the hides and sent the wool to the Eldorado Wool Mill and had blankets made to keep us warm at night. They made those blankets in return for half of the wool we sent them.

We had a good milch cow and chickens that produced plenty of eggs. However, for sugar, flour, coffee, and other staples, we were lucky that Papa and Mama had a grocery store in the Texas Oil Field at Iraan. Papa sent us the needed groceries and some cow and chicken feed. Without this assistance from my family, I dare not think of what the consequences would have been for our ranch and family. My neighbors, who needed food as badly as we did, always remarked when they saw my sister Glen arrive from Iraan with her car loaded with groceries, "Stillwells eat again!"

We often shared with our neighbors and they with us. We all grew mighty close in those lean times. One day my neighbor, Grace Lochhausen, came to me and said, "I have nothing to eat in our house. Otto will be home tonight after being in camp for three months with our goats. I know he's going to be hungry." I gave Grace three dozen eggs that Roy had brought in from the ranch. Grace later told me that they ate all of the eggs that night for supper.

Many stories could be told about those four dry years. Etched in my memory are so many, many sad and disastrous tales, although some are comical and on the ridiculous side. Nevertheless, those drought years will be repeated as time goes on, but ranchmen will be better prepared with all the modern improvements in electricity, transportation, and communication.

By the year 1934, some rains came, and with them hopes for a brighter future for our ranch. Roy and I stood on the sand pile and watched the geese fly north another time, an indication that spring was on its way. We had weathered the horrible drought and depression of the thirties but would long remember those days.

Winning My Spurs

THERE is never a dull moment in rearing children in the country, and I feel that I had my share of anxious moments. I often climbed to the top of the windmill to take a look over the surrounding country or climbed to the top of the sand pile to search for signs of my children when they were off and about the countryside. On the other hand, many incidents caused laughter and fun, so I always took things in my stride.

One rule that I laid down to all was what I called a "sundown law." I insisted that everyone be at home by sundown. I did not want to be worrying about anyone being out in the dark.

The first time I let Son go visiting alone, he went to see his cousins,

Jane, Dolly, Jim, and Stanley Henderson, who lived on the Henderson Ranch some five miles from our ranch. As sundown approached on that day, Son had not come home. I climbed the windmill to look for a sign of him. There was none. Roy was concerned but tried to calm my fears. He said that Son's horse would bring him home. I had just about reached the state of panic when I heard Son coming in a high lope, bawling at the top of his lungs. This was an indication that Son was all right; he was crying too loudly to be really hurt.

I asked, as he approached the house, "Why are you so late, Son? The sun has been down a long time!"

"I know, Mama," cried Son. "When the sun went down I knew I had to be home, but I forgot I had to come five miles, and I knew you'd be worried, and I'd be in trouble." Son learned a valuable lesson on this trip.

One hot summer day, not long after Son's visit to the Hendersons', Lee was late coming home. I knew that he should have been in early. When Lee finally arrived at the ranch much after dark, I asked, "What kept you so long, Lee?"

"I hate to tell you," Lee said. He had a pale and peculiar look about him. "I was real tired and hot when I came to the three daggers [a special landmark on the ranch], and I decided to get in the shade there and rest for a spell. As I sat down under one of the daggers, something pricked me. I glanced down and watched as a rattlesnake crawled out from under me. I knew immediately that he had bitten me. I couldn't see my behind, and I had no way to treat a bite in that particular position. I finally decided that it was best to just sit there and die. I knew that Roy and you could find me. I carefully propped myself against that dagger and awaited my death. I knew that the bite was fatal, and being all alone there was nothing I could do but just die."

I looked at Lee's ghost-white face and thought how awful it was for poor Lee to have felt that his death was so near.

Lee paused for some time and then continued. "I was not sick and did not feel any pain as I waited. I had cooled off a bit and felt as well as ever, so I decided to get up and ride home. When I stood up, I felt the pain in my rear again. I reached back and rubbed my fingers across the point of a dagger embedded in my skin. I suddenly realized that I had no snakebite, just the point of a cactus causing my preparation for death."

We both laughed a little and were glad that the incident was not worse than it was. Lee's horrible experience has stayed with me forever, and from that time forward, I cautioned my children to "look, and look good" for rattlesnakes when they got off their horses. I also cautioned, "Never, never sit down in a shade without searching the area for snakes, tarantulas, scorpions, or spiders." I also was glad that I had created the "sundown law." As time passed we were forever on the watch for creatures who carried poisonous bites.

When I wasn't looking for creatures I was facing one, it seemed. On one occasion, I had just put a pan of biscuits in the oven when Roy came into the house and asked if I could help him outside for a few minutes. I agreed and headed out the door as he told Dadie to keep an eye on supper.

Roy had a bull in the pen near the house and needed to look at an unusual spot or marking on the bull's rump, where he was afraid that something had bitten him. He had tried to work the bull for several minutes but could not get behind him. The bull refused to allow him to get close and Roy had become frustrated and came for me.

As we approached the bull he said, "Hon, you get around in front of him, and I will sneak up behind while he centers his attention on you."

I did not feel right about this situation and picked up a small stick to help protect myself just as I heard Roy say, "You don't need to be afraid, he's gentle. He won't hurt you – just ease up in front of him."

I reluctantly did as I was told. I faced the eyes of the bull and began to ease toward the center of his focus. I had not even taken my stand when the bull glared at me with fiery red eyes and charged directly at me.

My first instinct was to run, which I did, but not fast enough. Just after I split into my race for safety, I glanced over my shoulders and saw the gigantic horns close enough to gore me. At that moment, my legs turned to jelly and my body fell into a heap upon the ground. Visions of Lee preparing for his death came before me as I prepared for mine. I had dropped as though I had been shot and knew that the next blow would be the horns of the bull. Instead, Roy was one step ahead of the bull. He cracked his rope over the bull's head, causing the bull to turn from me and charge him. Roy ran to the fence, quickly climbed it, and escaped the gore of the bull.

While the bull's attention was on Roy, I managed to get life back into my legs and drag myself to the opposite end of the pen where I too climbed the fence for protection. I was shaking all over and attempting to catch my breath when I heard Roy yelling at me.

"Why in the hell did you fall down?"

I yelled back, "For the simple reason that I couldn't stand up!"

He just shook his head and eyed the bull. The bull was mad enough to fight a circle of saws at that moment. Roy roped him by the neck and snubbed his head tightly to a fence post. The bull couldn't move. Roy walked around to the bull's rump, investigated the spot, and released him. That's what he should have done in the first place, I thought. I got down from the fence and stalked to the house.

As I approached the yard, I noticed my children peering through the fence. They had seen everything and their eyes were filled with excitement and wonder. Son cried out to me, "Mama, did the bull knock you down or did you knock the bull down?"

I just glared at them and didn't try to explain. I passed them by and walked into the house.

Sometime later I told my friends, Mae and A. C. Spaulding, about my experience with the bull. They were horrified and enthralled by the incident. A. C. decided to write a poem for me that I have kept as a memoir of that frightening day.

> She was tall, good-looking, and some cowhand
> And she rode on her ranch on the Rio Grande.
>
> She wore a cowboy hat and spurs on her boots
> And a quirt on her wrist and she sure looked cute.
>
> You could hardly call her a cowgirl in full
> For just one reason – she was afraid of a bull.
>
> Then they went into the pen to look the bunch over
> And a bull took a look over his shoulder.
>
> And said to himself, "What's this I see?"
> That don't look like a cowboy to me!
>
> He gave a snort then she started to run
> The men of course were watching the fun.
>
> She slipped and went down in a desperate dash
> Then was up on her feet as quick as a flash.
>
> And she slipped again and went to her knees
> But she cleared that fence with the greatest of ease.
>
> Then over the fence and looking through
> She said to the bull, "To hell with you!"
>
> He snorted again in his bullish way
> And looked at her as if to say,
>
> "I'm boss of this herd, you'll understand
> I'm a fightin' bull – no Ferdinand!"

There was no end to our close calls while living on the ranch. Roy had taken one of our mean bulls to Dove Mountain to get him away from headquarters, because he was always causing a disturbance of some kind. That bull did not like living at Dove Mountain, so he crawled through several fences and returned to the chap (a small pasture) at the house. Roy and I did not know that the bull had returned until, to our horror, we both saw him at the same time charge Guy. I was standing in the kitchen door and Roy was some five yards away from the windmill. Guy had taken off in a run to join his father at the mill. Evidently, the bull saw the running child and came at Guy ready for the kill. When Guy saw the bull, he just froze in his tracks. The bull was at full charge and had his head lowered ready for the gore. Because Guy stopped in the nick of time, the bull's horns swept past him just inches away. Had Guy kept running, the bull would have had Guy locked in his horns. It all happened so quickly that Roy and I just gasped as we witnessed the narrow escape of our child. Needless to say, the bull was shipped out the next day.

On the Stillwell Ranch, March winds are always strong and many times blow for days at a time. We call the winds "good windmill weather" until they cause the mills to break down. These breakdowns usually always occur at a bad time – when tanks are beginning to bog, baby calves are being born, cattle are being treated and watched for screw-worms, and so on. At one point, we had such a breakdown. Roy sent me to Marathon during a high dusty March wind to get a new part for the mill that was broken. The trip was slow and long because the dust was thick and visibility was little to none on the road. I managed to get to town, get the part, and return that day.

The wind was still blowing when I returned. As I drove up to the house, I saw Son on the tip-top of the windmill working while Roy sat on the tank dump below giving him instructions. I was both horrified and panicked. I jumped from the vehicle and ran up to Roy shouting, "Why in the world is Son on top of that windmill? Don't you know he can be blown off and killed?"

"Better for him than me," Roy said as he smiled.

I was so angry that I could have pushed him into the tank of water. I glared at him and told him to get Son down. I wanted him safely on the ground.

I later realized that Roy knew that Son could hold on and do what was necessary to the mill so that we could continue to have well water for the house and cattle. It took some time but I finally settled down after a few hours and by sundown all was quiet on our "western front." I accepted the incident as I did all our incidents as being "all in a day's work" with Roy on the ranch. Although I silently questioned Roy and his ways often, I never lost my trust in him.

We had at that time a milch cow named Jane. I always did the milking because I wanted clean milk for my family. Men often paid little attention to how milk looked; they were usually just concerned about getting it. Roy did not like to milk and I really didn't mind, so the job had become mine. We kept a pile of sotol in the corner of the pen where we milked her, and we would feed her as we did the milking. One night we were blessed with a little shower and her stack of sotol got wet. The next evening when I went to milk the old cow, I turned her calf into her first. I watched as the calf approached its mother. The old cow glared at her calf and refused to let her suck. The calf tried again and again, but the old cow rolled her eyes and staggered up against the fence. When I tried to get close to her she would just sway around. I realized something was wrong, and I didn't want to get too close for fear that she might fall on me. I knew I had to get help.

I went into the house and told Roy that something was wrong with Old Jane. I explained how funny she was acting and how she refused her own calf.

He just snickered and said, "Well, if she's been into her sotol stack and it got wet last night, she's just drunk. That stuff ferments real fast."

This was my first experience, and not my last, with a drunk cow. As I think back, I do remember that she was just as obnoxious as any drunk man. The incident was yet another learning experience for me.

I would often be offended when Roy would yell instructions to me expecting me to know exactly what he needed. I told Mrs. Buttrill one day that Roy yelled at me a lot, and I was having a pretty hard time dealing with it. I whimpered that I was trying to learn as much as I could but sometimes it was extremely difficult. I remember Mrs. Buttrill just smiling at me. It wasn't until later that I understood her smile.

Once, when we took a bunch of cattle to Marathon for shipping, we stopped at the Buttrills on the return trip. We were all sitting around the table visiting and Margaret asked me in front of Roy, "Hallie, how did you get along on the work? Did Roy yell at you?"

I softly answered, "Well, I guess I did pretty well. Roy only yelled at me one time."

Roy interjected, "Now, just when did I yell at you?"

"Don't you remember when we started to put the herd through the gate as we left the ranch and you yelled, 'Get on the point!'"

"Yes," he said. "And you got up there fast, too! If I had said, 'Dear, will you please get up there on the point,' we would have lost the whole damn herd!" Roy looked at me and then at Margaret and said, "She didn't look back or anything when I yelled at her. She put her spurs to her horse and got on the point and we put the herd through the gate without any trouble."

We all understood one another a little better after that. Roy always seemed to have a reason for everything, and most of his reasons really did make sense once we talked about them.

There were many times when he never gave me any instruction. We would be gathering cattle and Roy would take off with only these parting words: "Take 'em on!"

Often I had no idea *where* to take them. I would wander around until I felt I was doing the right thing. I soon learned to read Roy's motions and I followed my own intuition; somehow, I nearly always made the best choices. I did learn quickly that he was a man of few words, and I figured out that I had to judge every sign he made for myself, and this way I learned more than anyone could have ever taught me. From this knowledge I was able to build and keep our ranch.

Recovery

RECOVERY from the drought and depression was slow and there was plenty of hard work. Roy and I didn't mind the hard work; we had become accustomed to that. I told Roy, and he agreed, that we should do many things to change our ranching operation. First off, I wanted to teach all our cattle to eat cake. I felt that we could have saved more cows from starvation had they known how to eat something other than grass. Next, I wanted to have gentler cattle, ones that wouldn't run wild at the sight of a person or a bouquet of red flowers – something many of our stock did during the hard times. I suggested too that we fence smaller pastures and ride among our stock more often. And we both agreed that we should have more well water on permanent watering places in case surface tanks went dry, a frequent occurrence during the drought. I knew that all these things were big orders, but I also knew that we could accomplish these goals if we worked hard.

Roy felt that we had suffered much, and he needed to replenish our stock, especially our horses. We had even sold three of our horses to the national park. Roy always took good care of his horses and refused to overwork or override any one of them. He knew that we needed horses and he would only have the best. Roy had been riding several horses: Orb, a horse he didn't like; Manchow, one Roy thought had to be pampered all the time; and Streak, a horse that was dependable but just not exactly what Roy wanted.

Roy was really looking for a special horse, a white one, one that he could call his own. He was talking to Roy Barksdale, a rancher from Dryden, one day and Barksdale told Roy that he had a mare that had just had a pure white colt. He told Roy that he needed a bull and would be willing to trade. The deal was made.

Some weeks later, Barksdale showed up at the ranch with mare and colt to trade for a bull. Roy was somewhat upset because he didn't want the old mare – he just wanted that white colt. But the colt was still suckling so Roy accepted the pair and Barksdale left with his bull.

Guy was about twelve years old at this time and was excited about the beautiful white colt. He would romp and play with that colt as though it were a playmate. I watched from the arbor often as the two frolicked in the pastures; one would kick at the other and then they would trade kicks. I think Guy thought of this colt as his brother.

Once the colt grew to about nine months, he was able to overpower Guy. Many a day, Guy would race for the house and protection from that colt. Still it was a challenge and pastime for Guy. As the colt aged, tiny red patches of hair appeared on his body and Roy thus called the colt Red, a name that stayed with him.

Once Guy realized that Red could overpower him and he was losing all the games, Guy decided to break him. And that he did. In a short time, Guy had Red broken and was riding him all over the ranch. Once he was broken, Roy took one look at him and knew that he was going to be a fine horse. Red was as smart as any horse we ever had on the ranch. I guess we all knew that from the way he played with Guy but never hurt him. Once Roy took over Red, that horse developed the same ranch sense that Roy had, and Roy was as proud of Red as he was of his children.

During school terms, I had to divide my time between ranch and town. In town, I attended social events and enjoyed the association of many women. However, most weekends and vacations were spent on the ranch. Roy came in to town as often as he could, and we went to dances, picnics, and rodeos together.

As our children advanced in school and there were more and more

17. Roy on Old Red, his favorite cow horse

activities in which they could take part, I found myself getting more involved in town functions. I became active in the PTA and helped with fund-raising activities. Then, before long I was asked to join with Mrs. Waddy Burnham and run for a position on the school board. She and I were elected, the first women in Marathon to hold the position of school trustees. I was interested in my children getting a good education and I held this position for thirteen years, but Mrs. Burnham resigned to take a teaching position.

I joined the Marathon Study Club and enjoyed being associated with the women who were working for the betterment of our community. One project that I took on was saving the first schoolhouse in Marathon. It had been long vacated and the town council was about to tear it down.

I headed straight to the committee to get the county commissioners to deed the old schoolhouse to our club. As owners, we borrowed two thousand dollars from the Marathon Bank to use for restoration of the building and landscaping the block of town where it stood. Many cake sales, dances, card games, races, and raffles were held to pay back this loan. In a few years, we had made a nice clubhouse, a community house for the townspeople, and a nice park in the middle of town for all to enjoy. I think this project was the beginning of my love for history and historical places, something that I have pursued throughout my lifetime.

As the children grew and the ranch needed constant upkeep, the demands for extra things increased, and my town activities also cost more. I decided to do something to provide a cash flow. I had always been handy at fixing people's hair and buffing fingernails. I opted to put in a beauty parlor in our house in Marathon and that gave me the extra cash I needed. I did have to acquire a barber's license, which cost one dollar. I cut hair, manicured nails, and fixed Marcel curls. I soon had money enough to buy a permanent wave machine. I worked in town during the week while the children attended school and on the weekends we all headed to the ranch to join Roy. We helped work the ranch and returned on Sunday evenings, when we would all gather around the radio and listen to "Amos and Andy." I became content with my life, my children, and my husband.

While my children were in their early years of school, Big Bend National Park was getting started, and I was curious to see firsthand the progress being made. I asked Adele Skinner, my good ranch friend, to go with me to take a look. We met a man in charge of the National Park Concessions who showed us the improvements being made in the area. He mentioned to us that he did not know where they would get wood for the fireplaces and wood heaters for the cabins and other buildings, since the park service would not allow any wood gathering in the park area. Immediately I volunteered to furnish wood and set the price at eighteen dollars per cord. I felt that I could make some cash in this way to help out on school and other expenses.

When I returned to the ranch I asked Roy, "What's a cord of wood?"

He asked why I wanted to know.

"I've contracted to sell wood to the park; they'll come here for it. All I have to do is cut wood into eighteen-inch lengths and they'll pay eighteen dollars a cord," I explained.

Roy's expression told me quickly that he was not happy about my new business deal, but he did offer to help. He said that a cord was a four-by-four-by-eight-foot stack of wood.

We hired three "wet" Mexicans to gather and cut the wood at a dollar fifty a cord. We borrowed a wood saw, hooked it to a back wheel of our truck, and were soon in business. With all of us helping we soon had a large stack of wood ready for the park. They bought this wood from us for several years. Later on, they installed oil-burning stoves, and I was out of the wood business.

Son was the first of our children to finish high school, graduating in 1937. About this time, Papa and Mama had sold their general merchandise store in Iraan and came to Marathon to make their home. Papa bought a house in the west part of Marathon, and I helped him with the remodeling and settling in. We picked up pretty rocks and Papa built a beautiful fireplace in their living room. I was delighted to have my parents living close by as they were a comfort to me, always very willing to help out in any kind of trouble or hardship. Roy's health was not good, and it was necessary for me to be with him more and more at the ranch to help him and Son with the work. Guy and Dadie would stay with Mama and Papa while I would stay at the ranch where I was needed most.

When Dadie reached her high school years, I felt that the responsibility of a teenage girl was too much for Mama. I decided to send Dadie to the Loretta Academy in El Paso. Guy remained with Mama and Papa. Dadie enjoyed her years in El Paso and graduated in 1938.

Dadie was then ready for college. I knew that Our Lady of the Lake College in San Antonio was a fine school, because Louanna and Marion Buttrill and Lucille Clark, all of Marathon, had attended this school. So, off to San Antonio Dadie went. In four short years, Dadie received a B.S. in physical education.

Son didn't really care for Dadie leaving home and he told me, "There we go sending Dadie to college, and when she gets out she'll marry some sorry boy and we'll be out all that money on her."

Roy didn't really see any need for the boys to get a college education. He wanted them to be ranchmen. He thought that they should learn the cattle business while he was able to teach them himself. He knew that they would some day need to take over. Roy was proud of his family, his ranch, and all the things that he had accomplished. My way of thinking – wanting more conveniences in our home – did not coincide with Roy's view of life. My friend, Margaret Hess, gave me her discarded kitchen sink when her family remodeled their home in Marathon. When Roy saw me unload the sink at the ranch, he exploded. "We're not going to put that thing in! We don't need a kitchen sink. I've piped water from the well here to the arbor, which is handy for you, and besides that, a sink is always stopping up, and I don't want to have to be cleaning out pipes all the time!"

"All right," I said. I hid the sink under the house. Every once in a while, I would drag the sink out in full view without saying a word to Roy. I was just mean enough to remind Roy that I still had the sink.

One day while visiting Tom Henderson of Marathon, Roy's great-nephew, I told him about the sink and my conflict with Roy. He just laughed. Then, a year or so later, Roy's nephew Gus Rountree from Beeville, who had come to visit Tom, heard about my sink. Tom told him, "Aunt Hallie has a kitchen sink and Uncle Roy won't have it put in her kitchen. She still has to carry water from a hydrant under the arbor into the kitchen."

Gus muttered as he smoked on his cigar, and then calmly said, "I'll put the sink in for Hallie."

We were all delighted and surprised to see Gus when he drove up to the ranch house and got out for a visit. After personal greetings and talking over the weather, cattle prices, and ranching in general, Gus said, "Come on, Son. You and Guy and I are going to put that sink in the kitchen for Hallie."

Roy looked at me. I looked at Roy. Not a word was said. We just watched as Gus took over and with our boys' help installed the kitchen sink. Gus stayed on a couple of days visiting and watching as I enjoyed my kitchen sink. I was so grateful to him.

Roy even enjoyed the kitchen sink as much as I did, and the drain pipe never did stop up or need cleaning. Once I had water in the kitchen, another thought cropped up. I said to Roy, "Save me some of those two-by-fours and lumber out of that old barn you tore down. I want to build a bathroom."

Roy staunchly replied, "I'm going to use that lumber to build a big corral. You've been complaining and wanted a bigger and better corral, so now I'm going to build it!" I accepted Roy's attitude and dropped the subject.

Finally, though, Roy began to see things my way and let me have the material I needed to build the bathroom I so desperately wanted. What a job it was, too. The lumber was old and hard, my saw was dull, and the days were hot. However, I sawed, I nailed, I sweated. Not a soul would help me. Sometimes I would need a specific board and wouldn't have it. I would go to the new corral, while the men were out in the pasture, and take a good board off the new corral and replace it with a bad one that Roy had pawned off on me. I would never tell what I had done, but Roy knew. He didn't say a word. He would just let me have my way.

By summer's end, my bathroom was finished. What a luxury! Shower, inside toilet, and hot water heated from a little potbellied wood water heater. You never saw a better-bathed family than the Stillwells. Roy took two showers to my one, and all again became quiet on the western front.

I soon realized that I would be spending more and more time on the ranch as the years went by, as all my children had finished school. There were fewer trips to town and I was needed more and more in the house. I contacted Bill Wright in Alpine, who was an agent for gas-burning refrigerators. I told him to bring one to our ranch for us to try out. I told no one about my order.

I was in hopes that Roy and the boys would be out in the pasture when Bill brought the icebox. But no, we were all sitting under the arbor, since it was such a hot day. We saw the dust and Bill coming with this big gleaming white refrigerator in the back of his pickup.

Roy jumped up and exclaimed, "What in the hell, now?"

Before I could muster up an answer, Bill was at our gate with the big icebox glistening whiter and bigger than ever behind him. "Howdy folks," said Bill. "How is everything, Roy? Had any rain?"

"Nope. It is hotter than blue blazes and dry as hell and you can take that thing right back to Alpine. We can't buy it!" Roy stoically responded.

"You can try it out, Roy. Won't cost a thing," Bill explained. "Come on Son, you and Guy help me, and we'll put this refrigerator in for your mama." The boys jumped up and started helping.

Roy turned to me and said, "Have you lost your mind? We can't afford to buy that icebox. You know how dry it is. Cattle prices are down and we don't have any money."

"Okay," I replied. "I'll go back to town to stay. I have a good icebox there. I am not going to stay here in all this heat any longer without a refrigerator!"

Roy didn't say another word. Bill and the boys installed the butane-burning refrigerator. We did get it paid for and enjoyed it very much. Roy was really proud of the icebox and would often brag to our neighbors about having iced tea and cold butter and milk on hot afternoons. He even said one day, "Why one can put a whole half-beef in it." He would tell how we had bottles of butane that kept it going. I always took a backseat and let Roy talk about the wonders of having a refrigerator so far out in the country. We were the envy of all the neighbors who would happen by. And that refrigerator was one more addition and improvement to our ranch. As I watched my children grow, so did I watch our lives and ranch improve.

With the good times came also the bad. Our boys had grown into men and were able to do most of the work around the ranch. Lee and Jona recognized this and felt that their days were numbered on the Stillwell Ranch. Roy would never have asked them to leave, but

18. Stillwell ranchhouse, 1940s

they, like Roy, could well read signs. They were both much older, worked more slowly, and appreciated their time more than ever.

Lee mentioned that he would like to go to New Mexico to live with his brother. Jona decided that he wanted to live in Marathon. One day they both voiced their ideas and I sadly prepared myself for what was to come. Lee left first. One day Roy came in and told me that he had purchased Lee's cattle, a herd that Roy had allowed Lee to build as he worked on the ranch. I knew then that Lee would be gone soon. It was a sad day when we put Lee on the train for New Mexico. He did not live long after he left us.

Jona was moving somewhat closer and his farewell was not as difficult. Jona got a small cabin in Marathon and lived by himself for several years before he died. We hated losing both of those wonderful men, but we knew we had to take another step in life.

Papa's Illness

IT had been a dreary day for me as I went about my daily chores. I couldn't seem to put my heart into the things that I needed to do around the house. Finally, I sought the comfort of my rock on the sand hill. Something was pulling me apart, and I couldn't get the usual comfort of my rock.

When Roy and the boys came in from the pasture for the midday meal, I said to Roy, "I don't feel right. I have a feeling that I don't understand."

Roy, who was always sensitive to my emotions, inquired, "What's bothering you?"

"I don't know. I just feel an impending doom hanging over me," I replied. "I think I should go to Marathon for a few days."

"Okay. Come back when you're feeling better," he said.

I gathered up my things quickly and loaded the car. I was headed for town in a short time. The ominous sensation persisted during the trip. I just couldn't figure out what was wrong.

Upon my arrival in town, I hastened out to see Mama and Papa, thinking they would make me feel more comfortable. When I got there, Mama informed me that Papa was ill. He had always had good health and I seldom worried about him. When I went into his bedroom, he was covered with blankets even though it was a warm day.

I asked my mother, "What's wrong with Papa?"

"Your father is having chills every few hours which have been going on since yesterday," she answered.

I immediately called Dr. Worthington, who came in time to witness one of Papa's worst chills. Dr. Worthington quickly examined Papa and was puzzled about his condition. He prescribed a medicine for Papa and started giving it to him immediately. Neither the medicine nor anything else we did for Papa gave him any relief. The chills continued. The doctor did not seem to understand what was wrong with Papa. He finally pulled us aside and informed us, "There's a new drug that has been recently released called sulfa. I've read about it in various medical articles and books. I would like to give this drug to Mr. Crawford but I'm not certain of its results. I'd like to get another doctor's opinion."

We agreed to send word to Alpine and have Dr. Malone Hill come to Marathon. Dr. Hill arrived in a few hours and the two doctors agreed to administer the new drug to Papa. We all waited anxiously, hoping and praying that Papa would experience some relief. But the drug didn't work.

During Papa's relief periods, he was coherent. He told us that he wanted to go to California to be with Doris and Alvin. He felt that the doctors out there could help him to get well. After much deliberation, planning, and arranging, Mama and Papa and I boarded the train and went to San Diego. Alvin had made reservations at a good hospital there and we had high hopes of Papa's recovery.

Very soon, however, even with the best of care and doctoring by the best of California's doctors, our hopes were dashed out. A short time later, Papa passed away peacefully. He had put up a good fight. I thought of what Papa had told me one time about death: "Daughter, death is God's will. It's not so bad. We're not supposed to live forever, you know."

Then I remembered back during a time when I was a teenager in Alpine. Papa was in great pain from an old rupture that he had suffered with since he was nineteen years old. Once, early in the morning, a siege of pain was more than he could endure. We called Dr. Middlebrook, the only surgeon in Alpine. He said, after a quick examination of Papa, "I'll have to operate immediately!" We were all shocked.

Since there was no hospital in Alpine at that time, we had to prepare for surgery right in our own home. We boiled water to sterilize the doctor's instruments, put clean sheets over the windows, and prepared our dining table for the operation. The only other medical assistant was Dr. Moore, who administered the anesthesia. Mama sat frozen in her chair with her eyes glazed over. Mabel refused to enter the "operating room," so she tended to the sterilizing of instruments, and I assisted the doctor with those instruments. I made a trail from the boiling pots in the kitchen to the "operating table" in the dining room. After such a trauma, we all were relieved to know that Papa survived the ordeal and soon recovered from the surgery.

I thought of Papa and his many fights for survival throughout this illness. But now there was no more fight left in Papa. Once the initial shock of his death was over, we had to plan for his funeral. Alvin took charge and quickly made arrangements for Papa's return trip to Alpine, where he was to be buried.

Once we had buried Papa, my life seemed so empty. Papa had always been my strength, someone I could always count on. I realized then that those strange and uneasy feelings I had experienced on the ranch were the forewarnings of Papa's death. I knew I would really miss him.

I wasn't worried about Mama. She was strong and I knew she would keep her grief for Papa to herself. She would grieve in her own way and she would carry on.

With Papa being gone, I found my "geese" flying about wildly. It was going to be much harder to gather them. Papa had always been a major part of my life, one who always helped manage everything I did. I wondered, "Can I gather my geese alone?"

As with most deaths, there is the sadness, the pain, and the loneliness. With Papa's death came events and traumas that took my mind from his loss. I was forced to pull myself together.

With war clouds gathering overseas in Europe and Japan, I had two sons to worry about. Hitler was ranting and raving loud enough to be heard all over the world. Roy and I would listen to our one-channel radio and wonder what our world was coming to. We feared for our family and home.

That fatal day came without warning – Pearl Harbor was bombed. I had barely digested that horrifying news when Son came bounding into the kitchen and faced Roy and me. "I've joined the service. Clifton Roark and I are leaving for San Antonio on the evening train. I want to be a gunner in a fighter plane and shoot every Jap in the world!"

My heart sank. "Wait a bit, Son!" I cried. "You'll be forced to go soon enough. Remember the draft!"

"I don't want to wait for the draft. I need to go now! I *am* going now!" Son exclaimed.

Roy and I knew that there was no talking to Son. He was a Stillwell. His mind was made up – there was no changing it. We put Son and Clifton on that evening train, wondering what their destinies would be. We just hoped and prayed they would get into a part of the service that wouldn't be too dangerous.

I waited patiently for word from Son but got nothing for several days. Then one afternoon Son and Clifton showed up on our front porch. They explained to us that they had not been accepted into the air force division that they had wanted to enter because they were both too tall to fly in fighter planes, Son being six feet six inches and Clifton just fractions shorter. The boys were not home for long, however; they were soon ordered to carry on to El Paso, where they would join the regular air force. Once again I suffered silently as Roy and Clifton headed for El Paso.

In a short time, we received a telegram: "Joined the Air Force, leaving for Biloxi Miss for training." I just sat and thought about those words. I didn't even get to see my son in uniform, although I imagined him looking tall and handsome. I knew that he would make a fine soldier.

As the days dragged on, Roy, Guy, and I kept the ranch going. We had to find ways to keep our thoughts positive, and that we did.

I tried to think of Son as a gallant soldier serving his country. I had to try to keep from worrying. I knew I had to be strong, as strong as Roy was being. I knew that he was hurting too.

When Son left the ranch, there was an empty horse. I had ridden little over the past few years because of my children. With the void in the ranch team, I decided to fill in. We were running some thousand cattle over an area of about two hundred sections and there was plenty of work to be done. One day I took Son's horse, his gear, and mounted, ready to work.

We became a team of three, Roy, Guy, and I. Our only hope of working such a large spread was through teamwork. With coordinated effort, the three of us kept the ranch going. In the evenings, I would be so tired I could hardly walk, but the first thing I did after a long day's work was turn on the radio and listen to the world news. I kept up with the war as closely as I kept up with my home and family. Son was in training for a year before he was shipped overseas, but I never got to see Son in uniform as he never was able to come home. I think he knew that if he came home, he might not want to return, and he was bound to serve his country.

With so much to do and so little help, we faced troubles constantly. We were working a bunch of cattle one day. I somehow managed to bungle my hold on a calf. Just as I had the rope secure around the calf, that calf reached up with its hind leg and popped me across the hand with a swift kick. Guy and I both heard the crack in my hand. I knew my hand was broken, but I knew that I had to hold the calf. Roy finally was able to relieve my hold, and I looked down at my hand, which was already swollen. I rubbed my hand a little, gathered my wits, and went for the next calf.

After a few more calves, Guy roped a pretty rough calf. I grabbed the rope with a hard yank. Just as I yanked, the rope slipped off her two hind feet and I took a bouncing spill, turning a flip on the ground. I landed just under the belly of Red. Had I landed under any other horse, it would probably have trampled me. Red, once again, proved just how smart he was.

By this time, I was bruised, broken, and disspirited. I gathered myself up with tears in my eyes and started for the house. About halfway, I stopped in my tracks. I thought of Son risking his life for all of us, I thought of Roy and Guy working so hard to keep our home, and I felt foolish. I twisted around, stood up straight, stomped back to the corral, and said, "I'm ready for the next calf!" I reminded myself that I was a survivor, not a quitter.

19. Hallie on Old Red

Believe me, there were times when quitting would have been so easy. We worked calves one day when I thought there was no way I could survive. Roy had penned two salty bulls that needed doctoring. Roy heeled the first one, Guy tied him over, and I grabbed a tie rope to tie him down. The first thing I did was put the rope on his front foot, and before I could jerk back he landed his back hoof right on my jaw. I saw stars and thought I had a broken jaw. Still I did not give up my hold. I attempted to secure the knot in the tie rope with him kicking and pawing. Just as I thought I had him, I realized that there was no knot at the end of the tie rope. It just slipped through my hand, leaving me with a royal rope burn in my palm. Being a person who is not prone to vile language, I shocked everyone within hearing distance, including my city sister Lovenia, who had come down to watch our cow works.

That night I crawled into my bedroll. We were working at Dove Mountain and the night was freezing cold. My head hurt, my jaw throbbed, and my hand burned. I had no medication of any kind, not even an aspirin. I talked myself into an uncomfortable sleep.

The next morning, everything was frozen including my body. It took three strong hot cups of coffee for me to think that there was any possibility of thawing out. I think Roy was feeling sorry for me, so he told me that he had discovered the tracks of a large buck. He said that we needed meat for camp and told me to hunt it down. I wasn't exactly enthusiastic, but I bundled up, loaded my rifle, saddled and mounted my horse, and rode off. The longer I rode the colder I became and the more stiff my body was. I had followed those tracks around in circles and never saw that buck. I finally gave up. We would have no meat for supper.

I turned my horse toward camp and started thinking about how badly Roy and I would feel when I returned with no meat. But there was nothing I could do; I just couldn't find the buck. I hung my head and let my horse lead me toward camp. As we were plodding along, I was startled by something directly in front of me. It was the buck. That animal jumped with such force and ran with such speed that all I could do was watch him in wonder. I never thought of my rifle beside my leg. I watched that buck until he was completely out of sight.

I slumped back into camp and told Roy the whole story, which was a mistake. I would have been better off if I had said that I just couldn't find the buck. He was really angry with me, and after that, I never missed bringing meat home or to camp when Roy sent me on a hunt. That time, though, I felt like I was a failure, and I know that Roy saw me as one. Once again, I chalked up another experience as one of learning.

Ravages of War

As the war raged and more and more Americans were sent to fight for our country, Roy and I worried about Guy being drafted. We were already suffering because we had so little help and we knew that we couldn't manage without Guy. On the Fourth of July one year during the war, we three were planning to go to Marathon to celebrate. Guy, of course being anxious to get there for early celebration, decided to go ahead of us. As we got ready to leave, we realized that Guy had not loaded the two-hundred-gallon empty container of butane for our refrigerator. Roy mumbled, "Guess Guy was too excited to think about his chores."

I told Roy that I would help him load the container and off we set to carry it to the truck. Roy tried to lift that bottle but could not budge it. I walked over to help him and the two of us couldn't move it an inch. We struggled and sweated over that thing until both of us were exhausted. Roy then got the truck and backed it up to a mound of dirt. We rolled that bottle up the mound, we took a plank and spread it from mound to truck, and rolled it into the truck. We both slumped to the ground in exhaustion.

Roy looked pathetically at me and said, "What the hell are we gonna do if they take Guy? Look at me. I can't even load an empty bottle of butane, and look at you. You can do even less. Damn, we're in sad shape without Guy."

I just nodded, knowing fully well that we had become dependent on Guy. I guess I realized then that Roy's health was probably getting worse and I was getting old. It took us a while before we could get our strength back and load up the truck.

Once we got to Marathon, Roy decided to drop off the butane bottle so Bill Wright could get it filled. As we drove into Bill's yard, he was standing on the porch. Roy told him what we wanted and he walked out to unload the bottle. He jumped into the back of the truck and started to move the butane bottle. He too had little luck moving it. He leaned over and grabbed the neck of the bottle and shook it. He stood up, looked strangely at Roy and said, "Roy, this tank is plumb full!"

The two of us looked at one another and laughed a little. We thanked Bill and jumped into our truck like two spring chickens. We weren't so old and helpless after all!

There were other indications of age, though, that I had to deal with. Son would write letters home and the government would censor them and reduce them in size. Well, those reductions were terribly difficult for me to read. I told Roy one day as I was trying to read one of Son's letters, "I'm going to San Antonio and get me some glasses. I can't read a word on this page." So I packed up and boarded the train to San Antonio.

On my return trip home with my new glasses, I found myself stuffed into a coach with people standing in the aisles. There were several soldiers who pleasantly stood as we women sat. As the trip went on, I and some other ladies began to share our seats with these soldiers, who were headed for El Paso. Our conversations helped pass the time.

We stopped in Sanderson for the crews to change and the new conductor checked our tickets and destinations. He asked where I was getting off and I said, "Marathon." He reminded me that that was the next stop. Of course I knew this; I had ridden this train often. The conductor left and that was the last time I saw him.

In the darkness of the night, the train pulled to a gentle stop and I assembled my belongings and headed for the exit. The nice soldier boys helped me off the train. I had purchased several things in San Antonio, so I had to organize myself before I could walk across the track to my home directly in front of the train depot. It was dark, I had new glasses, and my bundles were many. Finally, I had everything in my arms and I lifted my head to one huge mountain instead of my home. I quickly looked down the tracks as the caboose lamps flickered goodbye to me in the distance. I had no idea where I was. I was flabbergasted and lost my senses for a minute. Then I noticed a tiny building, something like a privy, with a lamp hanging in it. I suddenly realized what had happened. I had gotten off at Tesnus, a train switch station between Marathon and Sanderson.

I promptly grabbed that lantern and waited for the following train. I had watched and listened to these trains all my life. I knew that a troop train would be by in about thirty minutes. Well, I set myself in the middle of the tracks. As soon as that train came into sight, I started swinging that lantern. The train came to a screeching halt. I could see no one. The train was empty. Then from the far back, a brakeman started screaming, "What in the hell you think you're doing, lady?"

I explained my situation. He accepted my ignorance and told me to get into one of the coaches. He said when I got to Marathon that I was to pull the overhead cord and the train would stop. Then I would have to make a quick exit.

I got into Marathon at around four o'clock in the morning. Earl Young was the night watchman then and he saw me get off the train. He walked over to me and asked, "Hallie, what are you doing on that troop train?" I had to tell him my story.

I wasn't about to tell Roy, though. I loaded up my bags, walked across the tracks, tiptoed into the house, undressed, and slithered into bed next to Roy. What a nice and secure feeling it was to be next to his warm body. Roy never asked a question.

Later when I met people on the streets they would speak of my stop at Tesnus. I hurriedly reminded them that I had not told Roy and did not want him to know of my mishap. I should have known about the town grapevine. I held a large dinner party one night and had many friends for dinner. One in particular, Edna Verne Weston, had not been told to keep silent about it. In the middle of our meal she looked at me and asked, "How was your stop at Tesnus?" I just slumped in my chair and glanced at Roy. He was looking at me and waiting for an answer. I had no choice but to tell the story.

Roy just chuckled and said, "I wondered why you came crawling into bed at such an odd hour of the night." I knew then that Roy always knew what was going on. He just let me tell him in my own good time. We laughed about this often as we thought back over some of my big blunders.

I often thought of how many times I had "flubbed the dub" since I had been married to Roy. As Guy grew, I saw myself coming out in him. Somehow he could "rearrange" a deal as quickly as I could and I worried about this.

It had not dawned upon me that Guy had never been with us when we went after a "wet" Mexican until he failed to show up on time after we had sent him to the Rio Grande for one. We had let him go without instructions, and as I lay awake all night worrying because Guy had not returned from what I believed to be a perilous trip, I thought of the many cautions we should have given him. And, sure enough, he did all the things that he should not have done – innocently, of course.

After Roy and I had waited twelve hours after the time when he should have been home, we could stand the suspense no longer. We started out in the truck to find Guy. He and a friend, Emeral Martin, had taken the car so they could make a fast trip.

All the way from our ranch to the river we stopped everyone we passed and asked if he or she had seen anything of Guy and Emeral. From all the various people we questioned we found out before we got to the river that Guy had had car trouble and had to be pulled into town to have it fixed. Then we heard that he had made it to the river. One man told us that he had just seen Guy and Emeral and that they were sitting on the bank of the river and appeared to be waiting for someone. He told us that he had no idea when the two boys would be leaving their perch.

Roy and I hastened to the river, following the man's directions. We knew that there was trouble, but we did not know what to expect. When Roy and I got within ten to fifteen miles of the river, we saw an airplane circling overhead. After a few circles, it took off upriver. We continued on, and after we got farther down the road, we saw car tracks that obviously belonged to a *chota* (an immigration officer who prevented the Mexicans from crossing the river unless they had legal papers). Roy knew this because it was obvious that the driver had pulled off the road and backed up straight, perpendicular to the road, so he could see up and down the road by just sitting in that position. The tracks were so fresh, or "hot," as we often said, that we had just missed the *chota* by a few seconds. We looked ahead of us and noticed that a few hundred yards from those tracks were more tracks where a car had turned around rather rapidly; the tracks were wide and sand had been thrown all over the area. We then knew that the tracks belonged to Guy and that he must have headed straight for the river. Believe me, he had made tracks! They were still "smoking."

In a few minutes we came to the river and there sat Guy and Emeral, looking very innocent if a little "pale around the gills." They told us their tale.

They explained that they had been late getting to the river because they had had car trouble. When they did get to the river, the Mexican they had gone after was not there; he had decided to attend a wedding on the Mexican side. He left word for the boys that he would be back on the Texas side the next day. Guy and Emeral decided that since they had to wait for the man they may as well join in the fun. They decided to cross the river and attend the wedding. (I had failed to warn Guy *never* to cross that river.)

They hired an old Mexican man with a couple of mules to take them across the river and on up about four miles to where the wedding and a big dance was being held. They were quickly welcomed by the people and invited to take part in the "doings." Of course, the first thing they did was to obtain a bottle of tequila. (Another warning I had forgotten was: never buy liquor in Mexico.)

They drank a little and passed the bottle to others. They got along with that group of Mexicans quite well. The wedding started at about four in the afternoon and ended at midnight. Then the dance began. Although the Mexicans invited Guy and Emeral to dance, they did not. They had both been taught all their lives not to dance with Mexican women. This was the one warning that the boys remembered.

At the wedding dance, everything was going well for the boys until some Mexican soldiers from the interior showed up. These men had not been invited and were not expected. They immediately approached Guy and Emeral and wanted them to get some American ammunition for their guns. Guy and Emeral told them that they could do no such a thing. (Another of our warnings should have been: always say "si, si" when in Mexico!)

Their refusal to get the ammunition for the soldiers made the soldiers angry. Guy and Emeral thought that they would be nice and show these men some good will; they offered the officers a drink of their tequila. The leader of the officers took the bottle, started to take a drink, and then flung the bottle upon some rocks nearby. The glass splattered all over the surrounding area. Guy and Emeral were shocked. Guy and Emeral decided that they had better start for home. They began to look for their old man with the mules to take them back across the river and to safety. They found him and told him that they had to go quickly. But the old man was slow to comply, and Guy and Emeral began to think that they would have to spend the night and face being killed. While they were begging the old man to hurry, one of the officers walked up to them and began to converse with them in a friendly manner. This conversation kept the other soldiers from making any more trouble for Guy and Emeral. Shortly thereafter, the old man gathered up his mules and headed homeward with Guy and Emeral.

Just after the boys left the wedding reception, they came upon a trail that edged around the side of the mountain. There was an overhanging cliff just a few inches from their heads. This made for an uncomfortable trip home as they were hurriedly trying to escape the soldiers before they changed their minds about Guy and Emeral. Just as they rounded a large curve, a big rattlesnake lay in the center of the trail, all curled up and ready to strike. Guy told us that he and Emeral paid no attention to that snake. He said the snake could have bitten them both but they were not stopping for a mere rattler. They were leaving Mexico and those soldiers behind.

The boys made it to the river and got their feet soaking wet as they hurriedly crossed it. They then had to spend a few very cold and miserable hours in the car waiting for daybreak and an opportunity to get a little sleep.

When morning finally did come, they found the man they had come for and started home. The road was winding and very dangerous. They had just begun their trip when they came upon the *chota*. Luckily for the boys, the *chota* was out of his car looking at the airplane circling and did not see Guy and Emeral with their "wet" Mexican. But they were forced to turn around quickly and head back toward the river. (These were the tire tracks that Roy and I had seen earlier.)

Just as they were ushering the Mexican back across the river, Roy and I drove up. We went down to the river bank and called the Mexican to come back. We gathered everyone up and hastily headed up-river so we would miss the *chota*. We drove quickly to escape but shortly had a flat tire. We hid the Mexican in a nearby gully while we fixed the tire. Soon we were off again. After several miles, we had another flat; this time the mishap occurred out in the wide-open space. We had to search to find a bush large enough for the Mexican to hide behind. I began to wonder, "What else can possibly happen?" After the repair of the second flat, we headed home once again. That time, we made it safely with our valuable cargo.

It was after several such trips that Roy began to mull over something. I dared not ask questions. Then, one evening at the supper table, Roy announced, "I'm going to sell the Dove Mountain place. We can't handle it any longer with no help. It'll make things better for all of us."

It was said. It was done. Things were that simple for Roy. As I accepted the fact, I thought about the things that might have caused Roy to sell our second ranch home. Yes, there were good times and bad involved with Dove Mountain. I would really miss the place. It was a major part of my life with Roy, but I also realized that we had to move on with our lives.

A Teacher Comes Home

THE war continued and Son's letters were the joy of my days. He never complained, but he did miss a few things. He asked for such things as chili *tpins*, chili *gatas*, popcorn, and Planter's peanuts. Those we mailed to him quickly. The one thing I could not send to him was the wonderful smell of greasewood that he had told me he missed so much. I spoke of his desire one evening when Dadie was listening. She very promptly gathered some greasewood leaves and mailed them to Son. Of course, Son could not write about the war itself, but any news was always a blessing. He met a family in Cambridge, England, where he was stationed who often took him into their home for holidays and special occasions. I missed him, but ranch life continued.

Dadie was off in college at Our Lady of the Lake in San Antonio and loved the sisters and her studies. I had no worries of her wellbeing. She spent her vacations with us at the ranch but always promptly returned to her schooling, as she wanted to complete her degree as soon as she could. Dadie made many friends during her school days and often brought them home to the ranch for visits. We enjoyed almost all of them.

Only one time did her guest meet with disapproval from Roy and me. Dadie had fallen in love with a soldier boy and wanted him to meet the family. He was nice enough to load her up and drive her to the ranch from San Antonio, a one-way trip of over three hundred miles. We anxiously awaited their arrival.

As soon as the two got into the house, Roy took a disliking to the young man and instantly went to bed. He left me with the honors of entertaining a guest I was not so fond of either. The young soldier was a Yankee, and a "know-it-all," and did not seem to fit in to our West Texas way of life. I did the best I could under the strained circumstances, and I think we covered up Roy's reaction quite well. The young man didn't appear to be offended.

Dadie's visit was short. Upon her return to San Antonio, Dadie fell out of love as quickly as she had fallen in love. She had always been sensitive to her father's feelings, and I think that the visit indicated to her that the young man was not an acceptable mate for her. We never heard his name again, and the incident was never mentioned.

Dadie finished her college career in four years and returned home with a teaching certificate. She obtained a position in the Marathon Public School and in a short time was named principal. She loved her students and teaching and appeared happy and content with her life. I thought that she would pursue this profession for life, but once again I found myself watching my dreams dissolve.

Son had predicted that we'd send Dadie to college and she'd fall in love; instead she proceeded to fall in love with one of her students, Emeral Martin, a ranch neighbor whom we knew and liked very well. Teaching was dropped like a hot potato and held no interest for her any longer. We were disappointed, but we felt that Dadie was lucky to find such "good stock" in a man. Roy always felt that a person should come from "good stock." We were all excited. Emeral and Guy had been friends for some time and we felt that Emeral would in no time be a part of the family. The engagement was announced.

Because of the devastations of war and the dry times on the ranch, it was not feasible to have the big wedding that I had always planned for my only daughter. The couple drove to Del Rio, where they were married, and then enjoyed a short honeymoon. After that trip, they settled at the Martin Ranch, located near Santiago Peak some twenty miles southwest of Marathon. I was excited that my daughter was to be my ranch neighbor, but there was one problem. Her new home was not a cattle ranch; it was a sheep ranch. Roy wanted nothing to do with sheep and had said, "I don't want or need money bad enough to work with sheep!" Other than that, though, relations among the two families were good.

As time passed, Dadie became pregnant, and Roy and I were as excited about our first grandchild as Dadie was. I hoped that Son would be able to return and see his first niece or nephew. We were facing troubled times but found joy in many things in our lives. We held together and worked together.

Just as things brightened up for our family, the dark cloud hovered. Guy received his induction notice. He was to report to the induction center in El Paso immediately. Our heads hung low as we prepared him for the service. Roy and I were devastated, and wondered what we would do without Guy. But we had no choice in the matter. We would do what we had to do.

Roy and I put Guy, along with several other cowboys and friends of Guy's, on the train to El Paso. My heart was heavy that night. I watched as my last child was taken from me and then I slowly walked back to my house as the train pulled away.

Guy returned home just four days later. He had passed his physical and was told that he would have to wait about a week for his orders. The house was full of gloom. Guy was worried about Roy and me. He wanted to serve his country, but I knew that he was afraid that Roy and I couldn't "hold down the fort." He informed me one evening that he really didn't want to go "up there with those idiots." One of the officers inducting Guy had told him and his friends, "When you boys come back next week, leave your horses at home!"

In the days before Guy was to leave, we tried to keep our chins up, and Guy spent hours telling us the humorous events that had happened while he was going through the induction process. One of his friends, Fayette Yates, was being examined when the doctor examining him looked rather strangely at Fayette and said, "Did you know that you have a broken backbone?"

Fayette quickly responded, "Yes, I know it!"

The doctor asked, "Does it hurt you when you work?"

"Doesn't it hurt everybody to work?" Fayette gasped.

As we listened to those tales, we all relaxed a bit and our hearts were less heavy. Just a few days before Guy was to leave, we were all sitting around the table listening to the radio. The surprising and shocking news came: the war was over. Not only was Guy allowed to remain with us, but Son would be coming home!

Son Returns

I soon received word that Son was coming home. I felt that his return would make things better and that we could begin to put the ranch back together.

Son had never thought of being anything but a cattleman, and after three years of being overseas he was returning home to enter back into the ranching business with his family. Once he got to the ranch and saw how desperate things were, he realized that the ranch could not support us all. Drought, sandstorms, and relentless heat had devastated the Big Bend country for several years. Beef had become a most precious commodity on the American market, and it didn't take a tycoon to know that a lot of cash and credit would be required to make even a modest beginning in the cattle business. Son eyed his surroundings carefully and knew what he had to do.

Son had about enough cash left over from his service pay to buy the hindquarter of a good herd bull at the current prices. He didn't want to saddle himself with a massive debt by buying cattle on credit with the market fluctuating so. He knew a gamble when he saw one, and he was not inclined to gamble. Son knew he could use his G.I. bill and obtain a loan, but he had watched many a rancher wiped out by drought, blizzards, or screwworms. This didn't appeal to him either. He had to increase his capital.

Son saw that there was a demand for the candelilla wax, a substance obtained from the cactus that is native to the Big Bend area. Dozens of wax factories had mushroomed in the region around the ranch, and with the wartime price freeze lifted, the price of wax escalated from thirty-five cents to almost a dollar a pound. Son investigated the possibilities of setting up a wax camp at the Stillwell Ranch and deduced that it would be a profitable business. He didn't waste any time jumping on the "gravy train" with many other ranchers in the area.

He contracted a Mexican crew to produce the wax for fifteen cents a pound. An eight-foot *pila* (Spanish for *basin* or *vat*) mounted above an adobe furnace, a crock to hold the sulphuric acid used in the wax recovery process, a few barrels, a tin dipper for skimming the wax from the *pila,* and a dozen burros to carry the weed from the mountains were all that was needed to open camp. Son, at a cost of about one hundred and fifty dollars, had his camp set up to produce around two hundred pounds of wax per day. This grade and type of wax was bringing around forty-five cents per pound. On paper he computed stupendous profits. A profit of thirty cents per pound would net him sixty dollars a day, which was big money to any cowboy. Once he got his first factory started he planned to add an additional three. Son was in business.

When our tall lanky G.I. invested one hundred and fifty dollars in his wax factory Roy, being a pioneer cattleman, didn't mince words when he voiced his opinion of the subject of wax: "I'll be damned if I ever heard of a cowboy becoming a cattleman by making wax!"

Son ignored his father's remarks and continued with his wax making. Son soon heard from people in town, "That Stillwell boy is suffering from battle fatigue!" He knew immediately where the rumor had started. Roy just couldn't understand how Son could expect such foolishness to be profitable.

Still, Son continued with his wax production. He was realizing a nice profit, and with this profit he had dreams of establishing his own herd of cattle. However, Roy's silence was a constant reminder to Son that he was slightly out of paternal favor. I worried about their relationship and wondered if their old bondage would ever be restored.

From the time he was old enough to fork his first horse, Son had ridden a range that was thickly set with grey-green, pencil-like stems of the candelilla wax plant. Like Roy, Son had always considered the weed a nuisance because cows didn't eat it, human beings couldn't use it, and it wouldn't burn for heat. Now Son was looking at the plant in a different light.

Son sat astride his horse one day and viewed the beginning process of his wax production. He watched as a group of slow-moving Mexicans with pack-laden burros crawled across a mountain trail where no wheeled vehicle could have gone. From high up in the mountains, these Mexicans carried their valuable weeds to Son's wax factory nestled in a canyon far below.

Once the cargo arrived at Son's camp, the plant was unloaded and placed into the huge vats. There it was boiled like turnip greens in water acidulated with sulphuric acid. When the weed boiled it gave off its wax coating, whcih floated to the top of the vats. The wax was then skimmed from the boiling vats and placed in empty barrels where it would cool and harden. Once the wax hardened, it could be easily transported to market.

Son had watched the Mexicans use this crude method of wax extraction before he went to war but had paid little attention to the process. It was when he was overseas that he learned how really valuable wax could be and how many uses it had. He had heard Fibber McGee and Molly quip about the wax on the Johnson Wax Program that was aired over the radio, but these words had also meant little to him. Once Son became involved in the war, he was taught that all shells dropped from high altitudes were coated with this wax to prevent premature explosion. Airplane wings were protected with this same wax, as were tents, food packages, coats, and flying gear. Son began to realize that this particular wax had played an important role in his well-being and he returned with confidence that it would be a major commodity in the future market.

As Son worked, Roy was able to see some positive results of the wax business. He told me one day, "Well, at least I'm getting all that damned weed cut and out of the way since it's no use to anyone anyway!"

I just smiled a little to see Roy trying to manipulate himself into a positive mood about Son's wax business. I knew that this was a good step.

Son continued working as much as eighteen hours a day. He finally had three wax factories going full blast. However, actual production wasn't as easy as it looked on paper or from the sidelines, for he met all the usual difficulties that result from inexperience, unskilled labor, and remoteness from market. He used "wet" Mexican labor, and these men were geniuses at thinking up ways to stop work. They needed their siesta, they needed a drink, they had to discuss the boiling vats, they asked about one another's relatives, or they discussed ways to make the production faster.

As the men got the factory started one day, one of the Mexicans had a brilliant idea. Son had brought a can of gasoline to the camp just as a possible needed supply. This particular Mexican man noticed it and decided to help speed up the boiling process. He threw the entire can on the fire below a vat. In seconds, the camp was destroyed in a brilliant display of fireworks, the burros stampeded all over the mountainside, and men scampered behind rocks, into catclaw, and under bushes. Wax production in that camp was stopped for two weeks.

On another occasion, the foreman of one of Son's camps got word through the "river telegraph" (the Rio Grande grapevine) that his grandmother had died. Needless to say, all of the men wanted to attend the funeral. Son, being so understanding, granted the men permission to leave, and he headed into Marathon to attempt to get a skeleton crew to keep production going. Upon Son's return to camp, he discovered that the original crew had departed with all the burros, camp equipment, and a ninety-dollar stockpile of groceries. Those men never came back.

Along with the labor problems came the problem of water, a most precious commodity in the area. Rainfall declined as wax production increased, and soon all of the nearby water tanks were dry. Because of this Son had to have water hauled from great distances. Yet even so, profits increased. Son was making money.

Once Son had pocketed a goodly sum of money, an amount Roy expected him to spend on cattle, he purchased a bulldozer, a heavy truck, and some farm machinery. Roy didn't have "battle fatigue" to blame this mess on. He just clammed up and pretended that Son wasn't around.

With his tractor, Son cultivated a large tract of land that was to be planted in feed (maize, or corn) when the rains came. Then he built roads to remote sections of the ranch, making travel possible by truck so that saddle horses could be transported to isolated regions, thus saving days of riding time. He built dams and ditches to bring overflow water to the cultivated lands. He also built tanks and roads on the ranch, as well as for neighboring ranchers, who paid him well for his work. Roy began to notice Son again.

The rain, however, never came. Son's ditches and dams lay starving for the fulfillment of the cool water. Son tried to keep his hopes high, envisioning a new style of ranching with most of the work done by machines. But the rains seemed to be against him and slowly his dream of being a cattle rancher became a dissipating mirage.

The sun rose in a fiery blaze each morning and rode across the pale blue sky as a steaming ball. Son watched as the sky filled with speckly scavengers searching out the dying or dead animals that could not survive the drought. What water there had been in tanks and streams receded nonchalantly as man and beast stood by helplessly. Son knew that he could no longer provide water to his profitable wax factories. He would have to shut them down.

He told me of the day he had made his decision. As he approached one of our tanks to get a load of water for the factories, he found Roy frantically fanning the surface of the water with his hat. Son thought of "battle fatigue." As Son got up to the tank, he could not believe what he saw. Since the last haul of water some hours ago, the tank had dropped several inches. He looked at his father.

Roy spoke. "Son, this drought just about has us licked. I've been in the cattle business right here on this ranch for over fifty years, and this is the first time water ever got so low that I had to fan the bees and the yellow jackets off to save every drop of water for the stock." Son knew that Roy was jokingly trying to hide his desperation. Son just patted his father on the back and walked to his truck and drove off. He never took another ounce of water for his wax factory, and Roy never said another word about it.

In less than twenty-four hours after Son's decision, he devised another moneymaking scheme. Loading his bulldozer and farm machinery onto big cattle trucks, he moved up the Rio Grande to the irrigated farms in Tornillo, a village near El Paso. There he was able to work his equipment in the farms, making ditches and tanks, digging irrigation canals, excavating for barns, and levelling for house foundations. He kept his equipment running twenty-four hours a day.

Although Son was making money, his mind and heart were not focusing on his construction work. All he could think of were the fine Hereford cattle on the Stillwell Ranch that were sinking up to their bellies as they tried to reach the last puddles of water seeping into the earth in each dirt tank. He wanted desperately to be a rancher.

At home on the ranch, Roy made a decision that would affect everyone in the family: the cattle would be sold. The process began. Cattle that were too poor to move were kept and fed. The best of the herd were kept for seed cattle. The remainder, the majority of the herd, was sent to market. Once the cattle had been shipped, Roy felt no reprieve. The wind blasted across his now desert pasture, the sun pounded down upon the parched ground, and no rain clouds hovered above. The feed bills for the remaining stock were mounting and were soon higher than they had ever been. The ranchers in West Texas were facing the devil himself.

Son, working in an area of stock feed production, found a way to help. On the weekends, he shut his equipment down, loaded his truck with cattle feed, drove almost three hundred miles to the ranch, and unloaded. He slept a short time, ate a good meal and headed back to Tornillo, where he began work early on Monday mornings. Those loads of feed meant the difference between death and survival for those few remaining cattle that Roy refused to sell. Roy wouldn't let go of the ranch.

Son watched his family experience excruciating financial losses. Their sobering effect made Son a more determined man than ever. He continued his weekend hauls to the ranch where man and animal were precariously hanging onto life. On one trip, Son was caught in a wretched sandstorm. As he drove, the dust thickened and appeared to be suspended in the air around him. The wind increased and the dust boiled up as if hooves of stampeding cattle were churning the drought-dried land. The storm got so bad that Son could not see. He was depending on his truck to make its way through the maze of sandy particles. Time seemed to stand still and then, from out of nowhere, loomed the ranch house. With his bandana tied over his face to protect him from the driving sand, he jumped from the truck and ran for the house. Inside, Roy, Guy, and I were waiting out the storm. We had been worried that Son wouldn't be able to get home. His face was sand-whipped, his eyes were bloodshot, but he had made it.

Even as the storm beat upon the house the horses, tails turned to the wind, waited at the gate to be fed. The cattle milled around and bawled, but it was impossible to put out hay as each forkful would be whisked up by the wind and carried away. The sun seemed to be fading and the darkness intensified although it was only the middle of the afternoon. Even the chickens went to roost. Son went to the window and watched for a while as everything his father had worked so hard for was literally blown away. Then he turned from the window, walked to the kitchen table, and folded his massive frame into a chair. He leaned his elbows upon the table and dragged them to his chest, leaving a trail in the layered dust. He just stared at the dust on the table. I had put food in front of everyone, but no one ate. Anything, at that point, would have been full of grit. We just all sat in silence.

Finally, after a long silent spell, Roy said, "I'm going to bed." The rest of us followed. We shook the sheets carefully and watched as the sand dispersed throughout the hazed air around us. All I could think of was the last ripples of water in the tanks being carried away by the wind and spattered over the desolate ground where it would disappear. Our weak cattle would not have a chance against this storm.

Around daylight the next day, the storm subsided. We all bustled around trying to remove the sand from our clothes, shoes, and the house. We prepared to check the stock as soon as we had eaten. I had just finished my meal when the storm violently struck again with no mercy. For three more days, the region was ravaged by sand, wind, and heat. We watched as our cattle dropped in their tracks; there was nothing we could do. The carcasses of dead animals were covered with drifts of sand. The vultures could not even dine upon them. I watched in silence as Roy and the boys suffered quietly. After the third day, Roy looked at Son and said, "You were right not to put your money into cattle." Son told me later that that was the first time he had ever heard Roy say that money could be better spent anywhere other than on cattle.

When the storm finally let up, Son returned to Tornillo, but he was back the next weekend with another load of feed. Son just refused to give up on Roy or the ranch. He was as determined as any Stillwell. He told me that one day he would see his own herd grazing on the Stillwell Ranch. I believed him. Somehow, I knew it would happen.

Roy's Death

TIMES were getting tough once again as we had had little rain on the ranch. It had been about two weeks since the terrible dust storm and no relief was in sight. We had split the herd; Roy had moved some of our cattle to Black Gap, some fifteen miles from the ranch, because we didn't have enough grass or water for them. Son and Guy usually tended to the cattle on our ranch, and Roy and I worked the herd in Black Gap. We had had the cattle at Black Gap for several months when Roy and I discovered that they weren't looking well. We had gone down in the car to check the herd, when Roy got out and gave them a close inspection. We had driven right up to the cattle at the water tank where they usually grazed. After looking at each head, he turned to me and announced, "There isn't enough grass or water here to keep these cows in good shape. We'll have to move them back to the ranch where we can keep a close eye on them."

I expected that we would return the next day and round the cattle up and bring them to the ranch. I should have known better. When Roy made up his mind, action was immediate.

Roy shouted at me, "Hallie, you start rounding them up in that direction, and I'll start over here!"

I just looked at Roy. I had Emily Kay, Dadie's daughter, with us, because Dadie was expecting her second child. I wasn't sure what to do with her, but I didn't say a word to Roy. I just told Emily Kay to stay in the car, and I started gathering cattle. There we were, on foot, herding cattle down a road with a child in the car. I remembered Roy telling me that few men can herd cattle on foot away from their home pasture but if the cattle know that they are headed home, they will usually lead the way.

We were about three hundred yards from the car, and I began to worry. Roy must have sensed this. He walked back, drove the car up to the herd, got out, and started pushing the cattle onward. We'd move some three hundred yards farther, and Roy would walk back and move the car up. This went on all day. About dusk, we managed to get those cattle to the Stillwell fence line, where we pushed them to the closest water tank. There we left them for the night.

We were exhausted when we got home, and Roy and I just fell into bed. Sometime during that night, Son returned home with a load of cattle cake from Tornillo. He must have been as tired as we were because he also just fell into bed.

The next morning we were slow in rising. When I got up to start breakfast, Guy had already gone to feed the cattle and Son was still asleep. Roy, Emily Kay, and I ate breakfast, and I had just started washing the breakfast dishes when Roy announced, "I'm going into town to get a load of hay for the horses. We're running a little low."

I thought at first that I'd go with Roy, because I hated for him to make those trips alone. But I had to watch Emily Kay, who had already had an exhausting day previously, and Son was still asleep. I knew that Son would need a good breakfast after such a long trip, so I told Roy, "Go ahead. I'll see you this evening."

He asked, "Can I do anything for you in town?"

"Yes. Mail these letters and bring me two loaves of bread," I told him.

I later heard that Roy made the trip into town safely, got his hay, ran my errands, and made a last stop at the general store. While there, he was told that an old friend of his had just died. Roy knew that the old man had few friends, and he told Lucille Clark, the store owner, to be sure to order flowers for the funeral because we would not be able to attend. He left the store and stopped at our house in town.

Dadie was there. She reported to Roy that the doctor had told her to take it easy for the remainder of her pregnancy. Dadie told me later that she and Roy had quite a conversation. She said that Roy was really down.

He told her, "I don't think your Mama and the boys realize how serious this drought is."

"Oh, yes they do," she told him. "Mama just always tries to cheer you up. She realizes how bad it is. She knows we're in for rough times."

After their visit, at around four o'clock, Roy got up to leave. Dadie said that she felt that she should go with Roy, but her doctor had told her not to ride in a truck, because a rough ride could endanger her pregnancy. She really didn't want to let him go in such a state of depression, but she also had to think of her new baby. They said their farewells and Roy left with his load of hay.

Our neighbors, the Humphreys, showed up at the ranch at around dusk. I heard the car drive up and knew that it was not Roy. We were not expecting company. I met them at the door and Mr. Humphrey told me that Roy's truck, loaded with hay, had overturned and that Roy was badly hurt. He also said that someone had ordered an ambulance.

Son had already left for his return trip to Tornillo. Only Guy, Emily Kay, and I were there. I grabbed Emily Kay and yelled: "Let's go, Guy.

Your dad has been hurt." In minutes, we were in our car and on our way to the scene of the accident.

We drove up to the site. No ambulance had yet arrived. I jumped out of the car and ran to the truck. I saw Roy lying on the ground, lifeless. Someone had taken Emily Kay's quilt from Roy's truck and covered him. He looked so helpless. I just had time to lean over him when the ambulance arrived. The attendants moved quickly and had Roy in the ambulance in a short time. They allowed me to ride in the back with him. I had never been in an ambulance before. I knew Roy was breathing and there was no blood, so I felt that Roy would be all right. I never thought about death. Roy had always been a survivor and I felt sure that he would pull through this one accident. I was relieved that Roy was not suffering and expected the doctors to have him back at work in no time.

The trip to Alpine was quiet and fast. We took Roy straight to Dr. Lockhart's Clinic. Roy had always used Dr. Malone Hill for his doctor, but Dr. Hill was in Dallas. Roy and Dr. Hill had been good friends, and I insisted that Dr. Hill be called. The contact was made immediately, and although Dr. Hill was in an important medical meeting, he excused himself and called me. He said that he would get the next train to Alpine. I felt much better knowing that.

Roy lay unconscious on the examining table. Dr. Lockhart carefully checked him and shook his head. I was confused. I expected Roy to wake up any minute. Dr. Lockhart took me aside and told me he felt that Roy had massive internal injuries; his chest had been crushed, and he had several concussions. He told me that he thought that Roy had probably been thrown from the truck with tremendous force.

Just after I had talked to Dr. Lockhart, Dadie and Guy arrived. I explained to them what the doctor had told me, but they were just as confident as I was. After looking at Roy, they believed that he would pull through. There was no blood at all, no bruises, and no cuts.

Guy made the necessary telephone calls. In no time, Son was at the clinic, as were many of our friends and family. I am not sure that anyone believed that Roy would die. He was tough, and we all knew this. To us, he was invincible.

I never left Roy's bedside. I was waiting for Roy to wake up and talk to me. I thought of my last words to him: "Mail these letters, and bring me two loaves of bread." These were certainly not the last words I wanted to say to Roy. I had plenty of things to tell him: "Everything will be all right. I'll take care of you. We need you. Hang in there. I love you." I certainly didn't want him to leave me with only bread and mail as his last thought of me. I flatly refused to let him go.

I was so used to Roy and his silent spells that I felt that I should have been able to handle that one. Yet I knew in my heart that that silent spell was different. I didn't want to admit it to myself, but that silent spell was to last a long time.

About twenty-four hours later the nurse, Nettie Blevins, a longtime friend, was standing by Roy's bedside. She looked at me and quietly said, "Roy is gone." I just got up from my chair, walked into the lobby, and sat down. I remember Mrs. Burnham sitting beside me, but I said nothing. I just sat there staring into space. After what seemed like a long time, Mrs. Burnham turned to me and said, "Hallie, you're going to have to make some arrangements."

I stumbled through the following days as if in a deep black haze. We buried Roy in Marathon next to his mother and father. It was through Roy's death that I discovered how many friends Roy really had. I don't remember ever having seen so many people in one place before. Those people took charge; they cooked, cleaned, rearranged furniture to accommodate the casket in the living room, sat up all night with Roy's body, and helped in every way possible. It was good to have such friends at such a difficult time.

The drought and Roy's death had really taken a toll on our family and ranch. I was alone then and had only my children to turn to. And they too had their problems, which only worsened. The drought continued and we had cattle on the ranch that had to be taken care of immediately.

Sis and Gene Benson, good friends, were with me one day in my living room. Gene said, "Hallie, a lot of us are moving our cattle to Colorado to better grass. You'd better think about doing the same." Gene's parents lived up there and had found a place for the Benson cattle. I didn't know what else to do.

"All right, Gene. If your dad can find pasturage for my cattle, I'll send them to Colorado," I reluctantly responded.

Gene's father got pasturage for me very quickly. I think that Gene pushed him to find a place because he was worried about me. As soon as I got the word, I had to make immediate plans. We would have to round the cattle up and prepare them for shipment. Son had returned to Tornillo. He really needed his job, so I wouldn't call on him to help. Guy, an old Mexican man, and I rounded those several hundred head of cattle. I had ordered trucks from Alpine to pick them up and haul them to Marathon and the shipping pens. It was a sad day as I watched those cattle being loaded on the last truck. I felt that I was losing another part of Roy that day. Then, just as the truck was preparing to pull out, the clouds overhead rolled in with lightning flashing all around. Drops of rain trickled on my head and I looked upward. I could hardly believe what was happening. I started yelling at the men, "Turn them loose. Leave them here. Guy, go stop that truck! Don't let our cattle go!"

I had watched all the other trucks carrying our cattle away to strange and unknown places in Colorado, and I could hardly stand it. As each truck took a load of cattle, a part of Roy and me dwindled away. I had to hold on to that last truck, the last part of the ranch, the last part of Roy. I wouldn't let them take those few remaining cattle, all that I had left of Roy. I needed Roy to rebuild my life. I had to have a part of him. I stood screaming at the men, "Stop! Stop!"

Guy was able to stop the truck. The trucker looked at Guy, flashed a strange look at me, and shook his head. He geared that truck down, turned it around, and drove back to the pens. As he backed up to the chute, I walked with the moving truck and eyed each cow. I watched the men unload those few cattle in the pouring rain, and I knew that Roy was there with me, and with that tiny part of Roy, that minute herd, the Stillwell Ranch would endure.

In Memoriam

4

Hallie Crawford Stillwell,
1897–1997

After Hallie Stillwell died on August 18, 1997, just shy of her one hundredth birthday, the headline on her obituary in the *New York Times* identified her as a "rancher and a Texas legend."

As thousands of readers of *I'll Gather My Geese* know, Hallie became a rancher because she married one, Roy Stillwell, the epitome of the nineteenth-century cowman.

But Hallie earned the "legend" sobriquet on her own, during nearly five decades of hard work dedicated to saving the Stillwell Ranch. Roy's death in 1948 at the beginning of the longest drought of the century impelled Hallie to diversify. Having already mastered the roles of teacher, rancher, marksman, and mother, she became a justice of the peace, barber, journalist, author, storekeeper, R.V. innkeeper, and celebrity.

If, as *Texas Monthly* reported in its farewell tribute, Hallie was really "more representative of the New Texas than the old," Hallie and Texas are to be saluted, for enduring and evolving in enviable style.